The Constitution of
The State of Maryland:
A Quick Reference Guide

Bootblack Budget Books
Copyright 2018 ©
ISBN-13: 978-1986439961
ISBN-10: 1986439968

Contents:

Adopted by Convention – Page 4

Preamble – 5

Declaration of Rights – Page 6

Article I: Elective Franchise – Page 17

Article II: Executive Department – Page 22

Article III: Legislative Department – Page 38

Article IV: Judiciary Department – Page 75

Article V: Attorney General & State's Attorneys – Page 108

Article VI: Treasury Department – Page 114

Article VII: Sundry Officers – Page 119

Article VIII: Education – Page 120

Article IX: Militia & Military Affairs – Page 121

Article X: Vacant – Page 122

Article XI: City of Baltimore – Page 123

Article XI-A: Local Legislation – Page 127

Article XI-B: City of Baltimore - Land Development & Redevelopment – Page 135

Article XI-C: Off-Street Parking – Page 137

Article XI-D: Port Development – Page 140

Article XI-E: Municipal Corporations – Page 143

Article XI-F: Home Rule for Code Counties – Page 146

Article XI-G: City of Baltimore - Residential Rehabilitation & Commercial Financing Loans – Page 150

Article XI-H: City of Baltimore - Residential Financing Loans – Page 153

Article XI-I: City of Baltimore - Industrial Financing Loans – Page 155

Article XII: Public Works – Page 157

Article XIII: New Counties – Page 159

Article XIV: Amendments to the Constitution – Page 160

Article XV: Miscellaneous – Page 163

Article XVI: The Referendum – Page 166

Article XVII: Quadrennial Elections – Page 171

Article XVIII: Provisions of Limited Duration – 174

Article XIX: Video Lottery Terminals – Page 179

ADOPTED BY THE CONVENTION:

Which Assembled at the City of Annapolis on the Eighth Day of May, Eighteen Hundred and Sixty-seven, and Adjourned on the Seventeenth Day of August, Eighteen Hundred and Sixty-seven, and was Ratified by the People on the Eighteenth Day of September, Eighteen Hundred and Sixty-seven.

PREAMBLE:

We, the People of the State of Maryland, grateful to Almighty God for our civil and religious liberty, and taking into our serious consideration the best means of establishing a good Constitution in this State for the sure foundation and more permanent security thereof, declare:

DECLARATION OF RIGHTS

We, the People of the State of Maryland, grateful to Almighty God for our civil and religious liberty, and taking into our serious consideration the best means of establishing a good Constitution in this State for the sure foundation and more permanent security thereof, declare:

Article 1. That all Government of right originates from the People, is founded in compact only, and instituted solely for the good of the whole; and they have, at all times, the inalienable right to alter, reform or abolish their Form of Government in such manner as they may deem expedient.

Article 2. The Constitution of the United States, and the Laws made, or which shall be made, in pursuance thereof, and all Treaties made, or which shall be made, under the authority of the United States, are, and shall be the Supreme Law of the State; and the Judges of this State, and all the People of this State, are, and shall be bound thereby; anything in the Constitution or Law of this State to the contrary notwithstanding.

Article 3. The powers not delegated to the United States by the Constitution thereof, nor prohibited by it to the States, are reserved to the States respectively, or to the people thereof.

Article 4. That the People of this State have the sole and exclusive right of regulating the internal government and police thereof, as a free, sovereign and independent State.

Article 5.

(a)(1) That the Inhabitants of Maryland are entitled to the Common Law of England, and the trial by Jury, according to the course of that Law, and to the benefit of such of the English statutes as existed on the Fourth day of July, seventeen hundred and seventy-six; and which, by experience, have been found applicable to their local and other circumstances, and have been introduced, used and practiced by the Courts of Law or Equity; and also of all Acts of Assembly in force on the first day of June, eighteen hundred and sixty-seven; except such as may have since expired, or may be inconsistent with the provisions of this Constitution; subject, nevertheless, to the revision of, and amendment or repeal by, the Legislature of this State. And the Inhabitants of Maryland are also entitled to all property derived to them from, or under the Charter granted by His Majesty Charles the First to Caecilius Calvert, Baron of Baltimore.

(2) Legislation may be enacted that limits the right to trial by jury in civil proceedings to those proceedings in which the amount in controversy exceeds $15,000.

(b) The parties to any civil proceeding in which the right to a jury trial is preserved are entitled to a trial by jury of at least 6 jurors.

(c) That notwithstanding the Common Law of England, nothing in this Constitution prohibits trial by jury of less than 12 jurors in any civil proceeding in which the right to a jury trial is preserved.

Article 6. That all persons invested with the Legislative or Executive powers of Government are the Trustees of the Public, and, as such, accountable for their conduct: Wherefore, whenever the ends of Government are perverted, and public liberty manifestly endangered, and all other means of redress are ineffectual, the People may, and of right ought, to reform the old, or establish a new Government; the doctrine of non-resistance against arbitrary power and oppression is absurd, slavish and destructive of the good and happiness of mankind.

Article 7. That the right of the People to participate in the Legislature is the best security of liberty and the foundation of all free Government; for this purpose, elections ought to be free and frequent; and every citizen having the qualifications prescribed by the Constitution, ought to have the right of suffrage.

Article 8. That the Legislative, Executive and Judicial powers of Government ought to be forever separate and distinct from each other; and no person exercising the functions of one of said Departments shall assume or discharge the duties of any other.

Article 9. That no power of suspending Laws or the execution of Laws, unless by, or derived from the Legislature, ought to be exercised, or allowed.

Article 10. That freedom of speech and debate, or proceedings in the Legislature, ought not to be impeached in any Court of Judicature.

Article 11. That Annapolis be the place of meeting of the Legislature; and the Legislature ought not to be convened, or held at any other place but from evident necessity.

Article 12. That for redress of grievances, and for amending, strengthening and preserving the Laws, the Legislature ought to be frequently convened.

Article 13. That every man hath a right to petition the Legislature for the redress of grievances in a peaceable and orderly manner.

Article 14. That no aid, charge, tax, burthen or fees ought to be rated or levied, under any pretense, without the consent of the Legislature.

Article 15. That the levying of taxes by the poll is grievous and oppressive, and ought to be prohibited; that paupers ought not to be assessed for the support of the government; that the General Assembly shall, by uniform rules, provide for the separate assessment, classification and sub-classification of land, improvements on land and personal property, as it may deem proper; and all taxes thereafter provided to be levied by the State for the support of the general State Government, and by the Counties and by the City of Baltimore for their respective purposes, shall be uniform within each class or sub-class of land, improvements on land and personal property which the respective taxing powers may have directed to be subjected to the tax levy; yet fines, duties or taxes may properly and justly be imposed, or laid with a political view for the good government and benefit of the community.

Article 16. That sanguinary Laws ought to be avoided as far as it is consistent with the safety of the State; and no Law to inflict cruel and unusual pains and penalties ought to be made in any case, or at any time, hereafter.

Article 17. That retrospective Laws, punishing acts committed before the existence of such Laws, and by them only declared criminal are oppressive, unjust and incompatible with liberty; wherefore, no ex post facto Law ought to be made; nor any retrospective oath or restriction be imposed, or required.

Article 18. That no Law to attaint particular persons of treason or felony, ought to be made in any case, or at any time, hereafter.

Article 19. That every man, for any injury done to him in his person or property, ought to have remedy by the course of the Law of the Land, and ought to have justice and right, freely without sale, fully without any denial, and speedily without delay, according to the Law of the Land.

Article 20. That the trial of facts, where they arise, is one of the greatest securities of the lives, liberties and estate of the People.

Article 21. That in all criminal prosecutions, every man hath a right to be informed of the accusation against him; to have a copy of the Indictment, or charge, in due time (if required) to prepare for his defence; to be allowed counsel; to be confronted with the witnesses against him; to have process for his witnesses; to examine the witnesses for and against him on oath; and to a speedy trial by an impartial jury, without whose unanimous consent he ought not to be found guilty.

Article 22. That no man ought to be compelled to give evidence against himself in a criminal case.

Article 23. In the trial of all criminal cases, the Jury shall be the Judges of Law, as well as of fact, except that the Court may pass upon the sufficiency of the evidence to sustain a conviction.

The right of trial by Jury of all issues of fact in civil proceedings in the several Courts of Law in this State, where the amount in controversy exceeds the sum of $15,000, shall be inviolably preserved.

Article 24. That no man ought to be taken or imprisoned or disseized of his freehold, liberties or privileges, or outlawed, or exiled, or, in any manner, destroyed, or deprived of his life, liberty or property, but by the judgment of his peers, or by the Law of the land.

Article 25. That excessive bail ought not to be required, nor excessive fines imposed, nor cruel or unusual punishment inflicted, by the Courts of Law.

Article 26. That all warrants, without oath or affirmation, to search suspected places, or to seize any person or property, are grievous and oppressive; and all general warrants to search suspected places, or to apprehend suspected persons, without naming or describing the place, or the person in special, are illegal, and ought not to be granted.

Article 27. That no conviction shall work corruption of blood or forfeiture of estate.

Article 28. That a well regulated Militia is the proper and natural defence of a free Government.

Article 29. That Standing Armies are dangerous to liberty, and ought not to be raised, or kept up, without the consent of the Legislature.

Article 30. That in all cases, and at all times, the military ought to be under strict subordination to, and control of, the civil power.
Article 31. That no soldier shall, in time of peace, be quartered in any house, without the consent of the owner, nor in time of war, except in the manner prescribed by Law.

Article 32. That no person except regular soldiers, marines, and mariners in the service of this State, or militia, when in actual service, ought, in any case, to be subject to, or punishable by Martial Law.

Article 33. That the independency and uprightness of Judges are essential to the impartial administration of Justice, and a great security to the rights and liberties of the People: Wherefore, the Judges shall not be removed, except in the manner, and for the causes provided in this Constitution. No Judge shall hold any other office, civil, or military or political trust, or employment of any kind, whatsoever, under the Constitution or Laws of this State, or of the United States, or any of them; except that a judge may be a member of a reserve component of the armed forces of the United States or a member of the militia of the United States or this State; or receive fees, or perquisites of any kind, for the discharge of his official duties.

Article 34. That a long continuance in the Executive Departments of power or trust is dangerous to liberty; a rotation, therefore, in those departments is one of the best securities of permanent freedom.

Article 35. That no person shall hold, at the same time, more than one office of profit, created by the Constitution or Laws of this State; nor shall any person in public trust receive any present from any foreign Prince or State, or from the United States, or any of them, without the approbation of this State. The position of Notary Public shall not be considered an office of profit within the meaning of this Article. Non-elected membership in the militia of this State, a law enforcement agency, a fire department or agency, or a rescue squad shall not be considered an office of profit within the meaning of this Article; nor shall any remuneration received as a consequence of membership in a reserve component of the armed forces of the United States or of membership in the militia of the United States or of this State be considered a present within the meaning of this Article.

Article 36. That as it is the duty of every man to worship God in such manner as he thinks most acceptable to Him, all persons are equally entitled to protection in their religious liberty; wherefore, no person ought by any law to be molested in his person or estate, on account of his religious persuasion, or profession, or for his religious practice, unless, under the color of religion, he shall disturb the good order, peace or safety of the State, or shall infringe the laws of morality, or injure others in their natural, civil or religious rights; nor ought any person to be compelled to frequent, or maintain, or contribute, unless on contract, to maintain, any place of worship, or any ministry; nor shall any person, otherwise competent, be deemed incompetent as a witness, or juror, on account of his religious belief; provided, he believes in the existence of God, and that under His dispensation such person will be held morally accountable for his acts, and be rewarded or punished therefor either in this world or in the world to come.

Nothing shall prohibit or require the making reference to belief in, reliance upon, or invoking the aid of God or a Supreme Being in any governmental or public document, proceeding, activity, ceremony, school, institution, or place.

Nothing in this article shall constitute an establishment of religion.

Article 37. That no religious test ought ever to be required as a qualification for any office of profit or trust in this State, other than a declaration of belief in the existence of God; nor shall the Legislature prescribe any other oath of office than the oath prescribed by this Constitution.

Article 38. Vacant.

Article 39. That the manner of administering an oath or affirmation to any person, ought to be such as those of the religious persuasion, profession, or denomination, of which he is a member, generally esteem the most effectual confirmation by the attestation of the Divine Being.

Article 40. That the liberty of the press ought to be inviolably preserved; that every citizen of the State ought to be allowed to speak, write and publish his sentiments on all subjects, being responsible for the abuse of that privilege.

Article 41. That monopolies are odious, contrary to the spirit of a free government and the principles of commerce, and ought not to be suffered.

Article 42. That no title of nobility or hereditary honors ought to be granted in this State.

Article 43. That the Legislature ought to encourage the diffusion of knowledge and virtue, the extension of a judicious system of general education, the promotion of literature, the arts, sciences, agriculture, commerce and manufactures, and the general melioration of the condition of the People. The Legislature may provide that land actively devoted to farm or agricultural use shall be assessed on the basis of such use and shall not be assessed as if sub-divided.

Article 44. That the provisions of the Constitution of the United States, and of this State, apply, as well in time of war, as in time of peace; and any departure therefrom, or violation thereof, under the plea of necessity, or any other plea, is subversive of good Government, and tends to anarchy and despotism.

Article 45. This enumeration of Rights shall not be construed to impair or deny others retained by the People.

Article 46. Equality of rights under the law shall not be abridged or denied because of sex.

Article 47.

(a) A victim of crime shall be treated by agents of the State with dignity, respect, and sensitivity during all phases of the criminal justice process.

(b) In a case originating by indictment or information filed in a circuit court, a victim of crime shall have the right to be informed of the rights established in this Article and, upon request and if practicable, to be notified of, to attend, and to be heard at a criminal justice proceeding, as these rights are implemented and the terms "crime", "criminal justice proceeding", and "victim" are specified by law.

(c) Nothing in this Article permits any civil cause of action for monetary damages for violation of any of its provisions or authorizes a victim of crime to take any action to stay a criminal justice proceeding.

ARTICLE I: ELECTIVE FRANCHISE

SECTION 1. All elections shall be by ballot. Except as provided in Section 3 of this article, every citizen of the United States, of the age of 18 years or upwards, who is a resident of the State as of the time for the closing of registration next preceding the election, shall be entitled to vote in the ward or election district in which the citizen resides at all elections to be held in this State. A person once entitled to vote in any election district, shall be entitled to vote there until the person shall have acquired a residence in another election district or ward in this State.

SECTION 1A. Vacant.

SECTION 2. The General Assembly shall provide by law for a uniform Registration of the names of all voters in this State, who possess the qualifications prescribed in this Article, which Registration shall be conclusive evidence to the Judges of Election of the right of every person, thus registered, to vote at any election thereafter held in this State; but no person shall vote, at any election, Federal or State, hereafter to be held in this State, or at any municipal election in the City of Baltimore, unless his name appears in the list of registered voters; the names of all persons shall be added to the list of qualified voters by the officers of Registration, who have the qualifications prescribed in the first section of this Article, and who are not disqualified under the provisions of the second and third sections thereof.

SECTION 3.

(a) The General Assembly shall have the power to provide by suitable enactment for voting by qualified voters of the State of Maryland who are absent at the time of any election in which they are entitled to vote, for voting by other qualified voters who are unable to vote personally, or for voting by qualified voters who might otherwise choose to vote by absentee ballot, and for the manner in which and the time and place at which such absent voters may vote, and for the canvass and return of their votes.

(b) The General Assembly shall have the power to provide by suitable enactment a process to allow qualified voters to vote at polling places in or outside their election districts or wards or, during the two weeks immediately preceding an election, on no more than 10 other days prior to the dates specified in this Constitution.

SECTION 4. The General Assembly by law may regulate or prohibit the right to vote of a person convicted of infamous or other serious crime or under care or guardianship for mental disability.

SECTION 5. It shall be the duty of the General Assembly to pass Laws to punish, with fine and imprisonment, any person, who shall remove into any election district, or precinct of any ward of the City of Baltimore, not for the purpose of acquiring a bona fide residence therein, but for the purpose of voting at an approaching election, or, who shall vote in any election district, or ward, in which he does not reside, (except in the case provided for in this Article,) or shall, at the same election, vote in more than one election district, or precinct, or shall vote, or offer to vote, in any name not his own, or in place of any other person of the same name, or shall vote in any county in which he does not reside.

SECTION 6. If any person shall give, or offer to give, directly or indirectly, any bribe, present or reward, or any promise, or any security, for the payment or delivery of money, or any other thing, to induce any voter to refrain from casting his vote, or to prevent him in any way from voting, or to procure a vote for any candidate or person proposed, or voted for as the elector of President, and Vice President of the United States, or Representative in Congress or for any office of profit or trust, created by the Constitution or Laws of this State, or by the Ordinances, or Authority of the Mayor and City Council of Baltimore, the person giving, or offering to give and the person receiving the same, and any person who gives or causes to be given, an illegal vote, knowing it to be such, at any election to be hereafter held in this State, shall, on conviction in a Court of Law, in addition to the penalties now or hereafter to be imposed by law, be forever disqualified to hold any office of profit or trust, or to vote at any election thereafter. But the General Assembly may in its discretion remove the above penalty and all other penalties upon the vote seller so as to place the penalties for the purchase of votes on the vote buyer alone.

SECTION 7. The General Assembly shall pass Laws necessary for the preservation of the purity of Elections.

SECTION 8. The General Assembly, shall make provisions for all cases of contested elections of any of the officers, not herein provided for.

SECTION 9. Every person elected, or appointed, to any office of profit or trust, under this Constitution, or under the Laws, made pursuant thereto, shall, before he enters upon the duties of such office, take and subscribe the following oath, or affirmation: I, _____, do swear, (or affirm, as the case may be,) that I will support the Constitution of the United States; and that I will be faithful and bear true allegiance to the State of Maryland, and support the Constitution and Laws thereof; and that I will, to the best of my skill and judgment, diligently and faithfully, without partiality or prejudice, execute the office of_____, according to the Constitution and Laws of this State, (and, if a Governor, Senator, Member of the House of Delegates, or Judge,) that I will not directly or indirectly, receive the profits or any part of the profits of any other office during the term of my acting as_____.

SECTION 10. Any officer elected or appointed in pursuance of the provisions of this Constitution, may qualify, either according to the existing provisions of law, in relation to officers under the present Constitution, or before the Governor of the State, or before any Clerk of any Court of Record in any part of the State; but in case an officer shall qualify out of the County in which he resides, an official copy of his oath shall be filed and recorded in the Clerk's office of the Circuit Court of the County in which he may reside, or in the Clerk's office of the Superior Court of the City of Baltimore, if he shall reside therein. All words or phrases, used in creating public offices and positions under the Constitution and laws of this State, which denote the masculine gender shall be construed to include the feminine gender, unless the contrary intention is specifically expressed.

SECTION 11. Every person, hereafter elected, or appointed, to office, in this State, who shall refuse, or neglect, to take the oath, or affirmation of office, provided for in the ninth section of this Article, shall be considered as having refused to accept the said office; and a new election, or appointment, shall be made, as in case of refusal to accept, or resignation of an office; and any person violating said oath, shall, on conviction thereof, in a Court of Law, in addition to the penalties now, or hereafter, to be imposed by Law, be thereafter incapable of holding any office of profit or trust in this State.

SECTION 12. Except as otherwise specifically provided herein, a person is ineligible to enter upon the duties of, or to continue to serve in, an elective office created by or pursuant to the provisions of this Constitution if the person was not a registered voter in this State on the date of the person's election or appointment to that term or if, at any time thereafter and prior to completion of the term, the person ceases to be a registered voter.

ARTICLE II: EXECUTIVE DEPARTMENT

SECTION 1. The executive power of the State shall be vested in a Governor, whose term of office shall commence on the third Wednesday of January next ensuing his election, and continue for four years, and until his successor shall have qualified; and a person who has served two consecutive popular elective terms of office as Governor shall be ineligible to succeed himself as Governor for the term immediately following the second of said two consecutive popular elective terms.

SECTION 1A. There shall be a Lieutenant Governor, who shall have only the duties delegated to him by the Governor and shall have such compensation as the General Assembly shall provide by law, except that beginning in the year 1978 the salary of the Lieutenant Governor shall be as provided under Section 21A of this Article. No person who is ineligible under this Constitution to be elected Governor shall be eligible to hold the office of Lieutenant Governor.

SECTION 1B. Each candidate who shall seek a nomination for Governor, under any method provided by law for such nomination, including primary elections, shall at the time of filing for said office designate a candidate for Lieutenant Governor, and the names of the said candidate for Governor and Lieutenant Governor shall be listed on the primary election ballot, or otherwise considered for nomination jointly with each other. No candidate for Governor may designate a candidate for Lieutenant Governor to contest for the said offices jointly with him without the consent of the said candidate for Lieutenant Governor, and no candidate for Lieutenant Governor may designate a candidate for Governor, to contest jointly for said offices with him without the consent of the said candidate for Governor, said consent to be in writing on a form provided for such purpose and filed at the time the said candidates shall file their certificates of candidacy, or other documents by which they seek nomination. In any election, including a primary election, candidates for Governor and Lieutenant Governor shall be listed jointly on the ballot, and a vote cast for the candidate for Governor shall also be cast for Lieutenant Governor jointly listed on the ballot with him, and the election of Governor, or the nomination of a candidate for Governor, also shall constitute the election for the same term, or the nomination, of the Lieutenant Governor who was listed on the ballot or was being considered jointly with him.

SECTION 2. An election for Governor and Lieutenant Governor, under this Constitution, shall be held on the Tuesday next after the first Monday of November, in the year nineteen hundred and seventy-four, and on the same day and month in every fourth year thereafter, at the places of voting for Delegates to the General Assembly; and every person qualified to vote for Delegate, shall be qualified and entitled to vote for Governor and Lieutenant Governor; the election to be held in the same manner as the election of Delegates, and the returns thereof, under seal, to be addressed to the Speaker of the House of Delegates, and enclosed and transmitted to the Secretary of State, and delivered to said Speaker, at the commencement of the session of the General Assembly, next ensuing said election.

SECTION 3. The Speaker of the House of Delegates shall then open the said Returns, in the presence of both Houses; and the persons having the highest number of votes for these offices, and being Constitutionally eligible, shall be the Governor and Lieutenant Governor, and shall qualify, in the manner herein prescribed, on the third Wednesday of January next ensuing his election, or as soon thereafter as may be practicable.

SECTION 4. If two or more sets of persons shall have the highest and an equal number of votes for Governor and Lieutenant Governor, one set of them shall be chosen Governor and Lieutenant Governor, by the Senate and House of Delegates; and all questions in relation to the eligibility of Governor and Lieutenant Governor, and to the Returns of said election, and to the number and legality of votes therein given, shall be determined by the House of Delegates; and if the person having the highest number of votes for Governor or for Lieutenant Governor or both of them, be ineligible, a person or persons shall be chosen by the Senate and House of Delegates in place of the ineligible person or persons. Every election of Governor or of Lieutenant Governor, or both, by the General Assembly shall be determined by a joint majority of the Senate and House of Delegates; and the vote shall be taken viva voce. But if two or more sets of persons shall have the highest and an equal number of votes, then, a second vote shall be taken, which shall be confined to the sets of persons having an equal number; and if the vote should again be equal, then the election of Governor and Lieutenant Governor shall be determined by lot between those sets, who shall have the highest and an equal number on the first vote.

SECTION 5. A person to be eligible for the office of Governor or Lieutenant Governor must have attained the age of thirty years, and must have been a resident and registered voter of the State for five years next immediately preceding his election.

SECTION 6.

(a) If the Governor-elect is disqualified, resigns, or dies, the Lieutenant Governor-elect shall become Governor for the full term. If the Governor-elect fails to assume office for any other reason, the newly elected Lieutenant Governor shall become Lieutenant Governor and shall serve as acting Governor until the Governor-elect assumes office or until the office becomes vacant.

(b) The Lieutenant Governor shall serve as acting Governor when notified in writing by the Governor that the Governor will be temporarily unable to perform the duties of his office. The Lieutenant Governor also shall serve as acting Governor when the Governor is disabled but is unable to communicate to the Lieutenant Governor the fact of his inability to perform the duties of his office. In either event the Lieutenant Governor shall serve as acting Governor until notified in writing by the Governor that he is able to resume the duties of his office or until the office becomes vacant.

(c) The General Assembly, by the affirmative vote of three-fifths of all its members in joint session, may adopt a resolution declaring that the Governor or Lieutenant Governor is unable by reason of physical or mental disability to perform the duties of his office. When action is undertaken pursuant to this subsection of the Constitution, the officer who concludes that the other officer is unable, by reason of disability to perform the duties of his office shall have the power to call the General Assembly into Joint Session. The resolution, if adopted, shall be delivered to the Court of Appeals, which then shall have exclusive jurisdiction to determine whether that officer is unable by reason of the disability to perform the duties of his office. If the Court of Appeals determines that such officer is unable to discharge the duties of his office by reason of a permanent disability, the office shall be vacant. If the Court of Appeals determines that such officer is unable to discharge the duties of his office by reason of a temporary disability, it shall declare the office to be vacant during the time of the disability and the Court shall have continuing jurisdiction to determine when the disability has terminated. If the General Assembly and the Court of Appeals, acting in the same manner as described above, determine that the Governor-elect or Lieutenant Governor-elect is unable by reason of physical or mental disability to perform the duties of the office to which he has been elected, he shall be disqualified to assume office.

(d) When a vacancy occurs in the office of Governor, the Lieutenant Governor shall succeed to that office for the remainder of the term. When a vacancy occurs in the office of Lieutenant Governor, the Governor shall nominate a person who shall succeed to that office upon confirmation by the affirmative vote of a majority of all members of the General Assembly in joint session.

(e) If vacancies in the offices of Governor and Lieutenant Governor exist at the same time, the General Assembly shall convene forthwith, and the office of Governor shall be filled for the remainder of the term by the affirmative vote of a majority of all members of the General Assembly in joint session. The person so chosen as Governor by the General Assembly shall then nominate a person to succeed to the office of Lieutenant Governor, upon confirmation by the affirmative vote of a majority of all members of the General Assembly in the same joint session. The President of the Senate shall serve as acting Governor until the newly elected Governor has qualified. If a vacancy exists in the office of Lieutenant Governor, at a time when the Lieutenant Governor is authorized to serve as acting Governor, the President of the Senate shall serve as acting Governor. If there is a vacancy in the office of the President of the Senate at a time when he is authorized to serve as acting Governor, the Senate shall forthwith convene and fill the vacancy.

(f) When the Lieutenant Governor or a person elected by the General Assembly succeeds to the office of Governor, he shall have the title, powers, duties, and emoluments of that office; but when the Lieutenant Governor or the President of the Senate serves as acting Governor, he shall have only the powers and duties of that office. When the President of the Senate serves as acting Governor, he shall continue to be President of the Senate, but his duties as president shall be performed by such other person as the Senate shall select.

(g) The Court of Appeals shall have original and exclusive jurisdiction to adjudicate disputes or questions arising from the failure of the Governor-elect to take office, or the service of the Lieutenant Governor or President of the Senate as acting Governor, or the creation of a vacancy in the office of Governor or Lieutenant Governor by reason of disability, or the succession to the office of Governor or Lieutenant Governor, or the exercise of the powers and duties of a successor to the office of Governor.

SECTION 7. The Legislature may provide by law, not inconsistent with Section 26 of Article III of this Constitution, for the impeachment of the Governor and Lieutenant Governor.

SECTION 7A. Vacant.

SECTION 8. The Governor shall be the Commander-in-Chief of the land and naval forces of the State; and may call out the Militia to repel invasions, suppress insurrections, and enforce the execution of the Laws; but shall not take the command in person, without the consent of the Legislature.

SECTION 9. He shall take care that the Laws are faithfully executed.

SECTION 10. He shall nominate, and, by and with the advice and consent of the Senate, appoint all civil and military officers of the State, whose appointment, or election, is not otherwise herein provided for, unless a different mode of appointment be prescribed by the Law creating the office.

SECTION 10A.

(a) Except as provided in subsection

(b) of this section, a Governor may not appoint a person to an office in the Executive Branch of State Government during:

(1) The period between a primary election in which the Governor is not renominated or is ineligible to succeed himself and the inauguration of the next succeeding Governor; or

(2) If the Governor is nominated in the primary election but defeated in the general election, the period between the general election and the inauguration of the next succeeding Governor.

(b) In an emergency during the periods described in subsection (a) of this section, a Governor may appoint a person to an office in the Executive Branch that the Governor has the power to fill on a temporary basis upon filing a statement of emergency with the Secretary of State. Appointments made under this subsection are subject to the approval of the next succeeding Governor, who may remove the temporary officeholder and appoint a replacement.

SECTION 11. In case of any vacancy, during the recess of the Senate, in any office which the Governor has power to fill, he shall appoint some suitable person to said office, whose commission shall continue in force until the end of the next session of the Legislature, or until some other person is appointed to the same office, whichever shall first occur; and the nomination of the person thus appointed, during the recess, or, of some other person in his place, shall be made to the Senate on the first day of the next regular meeting of the Senate.

SECTION 12. No person, after being rejected by the Senate, shall be again nominated for the same office at the same session, unless at the request of the Senate; or, be appointed to the same office during the recess of the Legislature.

SECTION 13. All civil officers nominated by the Governor and subject to confirmation by the Senate, shall be nominated to the Senate within forty days from the commencement of each regular session of the Legislature; and their term of office, except in cases otherwise provided for in this Constitution, shall commence on the first Monday of May next ensuing their appointment, and continue for two years (unless removed from office), and until their successors, respectively, qualify according to law.

SECTION 14. If a vacancy shall occur, during the session of the Senate, in any office which the Governor and the Senate have the power to fill, the Governor shall nominate to the Senate before its final adjournment, a proper person to fill said vacancy, unless such vacancy occurs within ten days before said final adjournment.

SECTION 15. The Governor may suspend or arrest any military officer of the State for disobedience of orders, or other military offense; and may remove him in pursuance of the sentence of a Court-Martial; and may remove for incompetency, or misconduct, all civil officers who received appointment from the Executive for a term of years.

SECTION 16. The Governor shall convene the Legislature, or the Senate alone, on extraordinary occasions; and whenever from the presence of an enemy, or from any other cause, the Seat of Government shall become an unsafe place for the meeting of the Legislature, he may direct their sessions to be held at some other convenient place.

SECTION 17.

(a) To guard against hasty or partial legislation and encroachment of the Legislative Department upon the co-ordinate Executive and Judicial Departments, every Bill passed by the House of Delegates and the Senate, before it becomes a law, shall be presented to the Governor of the State. If the Governor approves he shall sign it, but if not he shall return it with his objections to the House in which it originated, which House shall enter the objections at large on its Journal and proceed to reconsider the Bill. Each House may adopt by rule a veto calendar procedure that permits Bills that are to be reconsidered to be read and voted upon as a single group. The members of each House shall be afforded reasonable notice of the Bills to be placed on each veto calendar. Upon the objection of a member, any Bill shall be removed from the veto calendar. If, after such reconsideration, three-fifths of the members elected to that House pass the Bill, it shall be sent with the objections to the other House, by which it shall likewise be reconsidered, and if it passes by three-fifths of the members elected to that House it shall become a law. The votes of both Houses shall be determined by yeas and nays, and the names of the persons voting for and against the Bill shall be entered on the Journal of each House respectively.

(b) If any Bill presented to the Governor while the General Assembly is in session is not returned by him with his objections within six days (Sundays excepted), the Bill shall be a law in like manner as if he signed it, unless the General Assembly, by adjournment, prevents its return, in which case it shall not be a law.

(c) Any Bill presented to the Governor within six days (Sundays excepted), prior to adjournment of any session of the General Assembly, or after such adjournment, shall become law without the Governor's signature unless it is vetoed by the Governor within 30 days after its presentment.

(d) Any Bill vetoed by the Governor shall be returned to the House in which it originated immediately after the House has organized at the next regular or special session of the General Assembly. The Bill may then be reconsidered according to the procedure specified in this section. Any Bill enacted over the veto of the Governor, or any Bill which shall become law as the result of the failure of the Governor to act within the time specified, shall take effect 30 days after the Governor's veto is over-ridden, or on the date specified in the Bill, whichever is later. If the Bill is an emergency measure, it shall take effect when enacted. No such vetoed Bill shall be returned to the Legislature when a new General Assembly of Maryland has been elected and sworn since the passage of the vetoed Bill.

(e) The Governor shall have power to disapprove of any item or items of any Bills making appropriations of money embracing distinct items, and the part or parts of the Bill approved shall be the law, and the item or items of appropriations disapproved shall be void unless repassed according to the rules or limitations prescribed for the passage of other Bills over the Executive veto.

SECTION 18. It shall be the duty of the Governor, semi-annually (and oftener, if he deem it expedient) to examine under oath the Treasurer and Comptroller of the State on all matters pertaining to their respective offices; and inspect and review their Bank and other Account Books.

SECTION 19. He shall, from time to time, inform the Legislature of the condition of the State and recommend to their consideration such measures as he may judge necessary and expedient.

SECTION 20. He shall have power to grant reprieves and pardons, except in cases of impeachment, and in cases, in which he is prohibited by other Articles of this Constitution; and to remit fines and forfeitures for offences against the State; but shall not remit the principal or interest of any debt due the State, except in cases of fines and forfeitures; and before granting a nolle prosequi, or pardon, he shall give notice, in one or more newspapers, of the application made for it, and of the day on, or after which, his decision will be given; and in every case, in which he exercises this power, he shall report to either Branch of the Legislature, whenever required, the petitions, recommendations and reasons, which influenced his decision.

SECTION 21. The Governor shall reside at the seat of government, and, from and after the fourth Wednesday in January 1967, shall receive for his services an annual salary of Twenty-five Thousand Dollars, except that beginning in the year 1978 the salary of the Governor shall be as provided in Section 21A of this Article.

SECTION 21A.

(a) The salaries of the Governor and Lieutenant Governor shall be as provided in this section.

(b) The Governor's Salary Commission is created. It consists of seven members: The State Treasurer; three appointed by the President of the Senate; and three appointed by the Speaker of the House of Delegates. Members of the General Assembly and officers and employees of the State or a political subdivision of the State are not eligible for appointment to the Commission. The members of the Commission shall elect a member to be chairman, and the concurrence of at least five members is required for any formal Commission action. The terms of members shall be for 4 years, except that the persons first appointed to the Commission shall serve from June 1, 1977 until May 31, 1980. The members of the Commission are eligible for reappointment. Members shall serve without compensation but shall be reimbursed for expenses incurred in carrying out responsibilities under this section.

(c) Within ten days after the commencement of the regular session of the General Assembly in 1978, and within ten days after the commencement of the regular session of the General Assembly each fourth year thereafter, the Commission shall make a written recommendation to the Governor, Lieutenant Governor, and other members of the General Assembly as to the salary of the Governor and Lieutenant Governor.

(d) The recommendation shall be introduced as a joint resolution in each house of the General Assembly not later than the fifteenth day of the session. The General Assembly may amend the joint resolution to decrease the recommended salaries, but may not amend the joint resolution to increase the recommended salaries. If the General Assembly fails to adopt a joint resolution in accordance with this section within 50 days after its introduction, the salaries recommended by the Commission shall apply. If the General Assembly amends the joint resolution in accordance with this section, the salaries specified in the joint resolution, as amended, shall apply. If the Commission recommends no salary change, a joint resolution shall not be introduced.

(e) The Commission may not recommend salaries lower than that received by the incumbent Governor at the time the recommendation is made; and the General Assembly may not amend the joint resolution to provide for salaries lower than that received by the incumbent Governor and Lieutenant Governor.

(f) A change in salary resulting from either Commission recommendation or amended joint resolution under this section shall take effect at the beginning of the next ensuing term of the Governor and Lieutenant Governor.

(g) Commission inaction or failure of the Commission to meet the requirements of this section with respect to proposing a change in salary for the Governor and Lieutenant Governor shall result in no change in salary.

SECTION 22. A Secretary of State shall be appointed by the Governor, by and with the advice and consent of the Senate, who shall continue in office, unless sooner removed by the Governor, till the end of the official term of the Governor from whom he received his appointment, and receive such annual salary as the General Assembly may from time to time by law prescribe.

SECTION 23. The Secretary of State shall carefully keep and preserve a Record of all official acts and proceedings, which may at all times be inspected by a committee of either Branch of the Legislature; and he shall perform such other duties as may be prescribed by Law, or as may properly belong to his office, together with all clerical duty belonging to the Executive Department.

SECTION 24. The Governor may make changes in the organization of the Executive Branch of the State Government, including the establishment or abolition of departments, offices, agencies, and instrumentalities, and the reallocation or reassignment of functions, powers, and duties among the departments, offices, agencies, and instrumentalities of the Executive Branch. Where these changes are inconsistent with existing law, or create new governmental programs they shall be set forth in executive orders in statutory form which shall be submitted to the General Assembly within the first ten days of a regular session. An executive order that has been submitted shall become effective and have the force of law on the date designated in the Order unless specifically disapproved, within fifty days after submission, by a resolution of disapproval concurred in by a majority vote of all members of either House of the General Assembly. No executive order reorganizing the Executive Branch shall abolish any office established by this Constitution or shall change the powers and duties delegated to particular officers or departments by this Constitution.

ARTICLE III: LEGISLATIVE DEPARTMENT

SECTION 1. The Legislature shall consist of two distinct branches; a Senate, and a House of Delegates, and shall be styled the General Assembly of Maryland.

SECTION 2. The membership of the Senate shall consist of forty-seven (47) Senators. The membership of the House of Delegates shall consist of one hundred forty-one (141) Delegates.

SECTION 3. The State shall be divided by law into legislative districts for the election of members of the Senate and the House of Delegates. Each legislative district shall contain one (1) Senator and three (3) Delegates. Nothing herein shall prohibit the subdivision of any one or more of the legislative districts for the purpose of electing members of the House of Delegates into three (3) single-member delegate districts or one (1) single-member delegate district and one (1) multi-member delegate district.

SECTION 4. Each legislative district shall consist of adjoining territory, be compact in form, and of substantially equal population. Due regard shall be given to natural boundaries and the boundaries of political subdivisions.

SECTION 5. Following each decennial census of the United States and after public hearings, the Governor shall prepare a plan setting forth the boundaries of the legislative districts for electing of the members of the Senate and the House of Delegates.

The Governor shall present the plan to the President of the Senate and Speaker of the House of Delegates who shall introduce the Governor's plan as a joint resolution to the General Assembly, not later than the first day of its regular session in the second year following every census, and the Governor may call a special session for the presentation of his plan prior to the regular session. The plan shall conform to Sections 2, 3 and 4 of this Article. Following each decennial census the General Assembly may by joint resolution adopt a plan setting forth the boundaries of the legislative districts for the election of members of the Senate and the House of Delegates, which plan shall conform to Sections 2, 3 and 4 of this Article. If a plan has been adopted by the General Assembly by the 45th day after the opening of the regular session of the General Assembly in the second year following every census, the plan adopted by the General Assembly shall become law. If no plan has been adopted by the General Assembly for these purposes by the 45th day after the opening of the regular session of the General Assembly in the second year following every census, the Governor's plan presented to the General Assembly shall become law.

Upon petition of any registered voter, the Court of Appeals shall have original jurisdiction to review the legislative districting of the State and may grant appropriate relief, if it finds that the districting of the State is not consistent with requirements of either the Constitution of the United States of America, or the Constitution of Maryland.

SECTION 6. A member of the General Assembly shall be elected by the registered voters of the legislative or delegate district from which he seeks election, to serve for a term of four years beginning on the second Wednesday of January following his election.

SECTION 7. The election for Senators and Delegates shall take place on the Tuesday next, after the first Monday in the month of November, nineteen hundred and fifty-eight, and in every fourth year thereafter.

SECTION 8. Vacant.

SECTION 9. A person is eligible to serve as a Senator or Delegate, who on the date of his election,

(1) is a citizen of the State of Maryland,

(2) has resided therein for at least one year next preceding that date, and

(3) if the district which he has been chosen to represent has been established for at least six months prior to the date of his election, has resided in that district for six months next preceding that date.

If the district which the person has been chosen to represent has been established less than six months prior to the date of his election, then in addition to (1) and (2) above, he shall have resided in the district for as long as it has been established.

A person is eligible to serve as a Senator, if he has attained the age of twenty-five years, or as a Delegate, if he has attained the age of twenty-one years, on the date of his election.

SECTION 10. No member of Congress, or person holding any civil, or military office under the United States, shall be eligible as a Senator, or Delegate; and if any person shall after his election as Senator, or Delegate, be elected to Congress, or be appointed to any office, civil, or military, under the Government of the United States, his acceptance thereof, shall vacate his seat; except that a Senator or Delegate may be a member of a reserve component of the armed forces of the United States or a member of the militia of the United States or this State .

SECTION 11. No person holding any civil office of profit, or trust, under this State shall be eligible as Senator or Delegate; however, a Senator or Delegate may be a non-elected law enforcement officer or a fire or rescue squad worker.

SECTION 12. No Collector, Receiver, or Holder of public money shall be eligible as Senator or Delegate, or to any office of profit, or trust, under this State, until he shall have accounted for, and paid into the Treasury all sums on the books thereof, charged to, and due by him.

SECTION 13.

(a) (1) In case of death, disqualification, resignation, refusal to act, expulsion, or removal from the county or city for which he shall have been elected, of any person who shall have been chosen as a Delegate or Senator, or in case of a tie between two or more such qualified persons, the Governor shall appoint a person to fill such vacancy from a person whose name shall be submitted to him in writing, within thirty days after the occurrence of the vacancy, by the Central Committee of the political party, if any, with which the Delegate or Senator, so vacating, had been affiliated, at the time of the last election or appointment of the vacating Senator or Delegate, in the County or District from which he or she was appointed or elected, provided that the appointee shall be of the same political party, if any, as was that of the Delegate or Senator, whose office is to be filled, at the time of the last election or appointment of the vacating Delegate or Senator, and it shall be the duty of the Governor to make said appointment within fifteen days after the submission thereof to him.

(2) If a name is not submitted by the Central Committee within thirty days after the occurrence of the vacancy, the Governor within another period of fifteen days shall appoint a person, who shall be affiliated with the same political party, if any as was that of the Delegate or Senator, whose office is to be filled, at the time of the last election or appointment of the vacating Delegate or Senator, and who is otherwise properly qualified to hold the office of Delegate or Senator in the District or County.

(3) In the event there is no Central Committee in the County or District from which said vacancy is to be filled, the Governor shall within fifteen days after the occurrence of such vacancy appoint a person, from the same political party, if any, as that of the vacating Delegate or Senator, at the time of the last election or appointment of the vacating Senator or Delegate, who is otherwise properly qualified to hold the office of Delegate or Senator in such District or

County.

(4) In every case when any person is so appointed by the Governor, his appointment shall be deemed to be for the unexpired term of the person whose office has become vacant.

(b) In addition, and in submitting a name to the Governor to fill a vacancy in a legislative or delegate district, as the case may be, in any of the twenty-three counties of Maryland, the Central Committee or committees shall follow these provisions:

(1) If the vacancy occurs in a district having the same boundaries as a county, the Central Committee of the county shall submit the name of a resident of the district.

(2) If the vacancy occurs in a district which has boundaries comprising a portion of one county, the Central Committee of that county shall submit the name of a resident of the district.

(3) If the vacancy occurs in a district which has boundaries comprising a portion or all of two or more counties, the Central Committee of each county involved shall have one vote for submitting the name of a resident of the district; and if there is a tie vote between or among the Central Committees, the list of names there proposed shall be submitted to the Governor, and he shall make the appointment from the list.

SECTION 14. The General Assembly shall meet on the second Wednesday of January, nineteen hundred and seventy-one, and on the same day in every year thereafter, and at no other time, unless convened by Proclamation of the Governor. A Proclamation convening the General Assembly in extraordinary session must be issued by the Governor if a majority of the members elected to the Senate and a majority of the members elected to the House of Delegates join in a petition to the Governor requesting that he convene the General Assembly in extraordinary session, and the Governor shall convene the General Assembly on the date specified in the petition. This section does not affect the Governor's power to convene the General Assembly in extraordinary session pursuant to Section 16 of Article II of this Constitution.

SECTION 15.

(1) The General Assembly may continue its session so long as in its judgment the public interest may require, for a period not longer than ninety days in each year. The ninety days shall be consecutive unless otherwise provided by law. The General Assembly may extend its session beyond ninety days, but not exceeding an additional thirty days, by resolution concurred in by a three-fifths vote of the membership in each House. When the General Assembly is convened by Proclamation of the Governor, the session shall not continue longer than thirty days, but no additional compensation other than mileage and other allowances provided by law shall be paid members of the General Assembly for special session.

(2) Any compensation and allowances paid to members of the General Assembly shall be as established by a commission known as the General Assembly Compensation Commission. The Commission shall consist of nine members, five of whom shall be appointed by the Governor, two of whom shall be appointed by the President of the Senate, and two of whom shall be appointed by the Speaker of the House of Delegates. Members of the General Assembly and officers and employees of the Government of the State of Maryland or of any county, city, or other governmental unit of the State shall not be eligible for appointment to the Commission. Members of the Commission shall be appointed for terms of four years commencing on June 1 of each gubernatorial election year. Members of the Commission are eligible for re-appointment. Any member of the Commission may be removed by the Governor prior to the expiration of his term for official misconduct, incompetence, or neglect of duty. The members shall serve without compensation but shall be reimbursed for expenses incurred in carrying out their responsibilities under this section. Decisions of the Commission must be concurred in by at least five members.

(3) Within 15 days after the beginning of the regular session of the General Assembly in 1974 and within 15 days after the beginning of the regular session in each fourth year thereafter, the Commission by formal resolution shall submit its determinations for compensation and allowances to the General Assembly. The General Assembly may reduce or reject, but shall not increase any item in the resolution. The resolution, with any reductions that shall have been concurred in by joint resolution of the General Assembly, shall take effect and have the force of law as of the beginning of the term of office of the next General

Assembly. Rates of compensation and pensions shall be uniform for all members of the General Assembly, except that the officers of the Senate and the House of Delegates may receive higher compensation as determined by the General Assembly Compensation Commission. The provisions of the Compensation Commission resolution shall continue in force until superseded by any succeeding resolution.

(4) In no event shall the compensation and allowances be less than they were prior to the establishment of the Compensation Commission.

SECTION 16. No book, or other printed matter not appertaining to the business of the session, shall be purchased, or subscribed for, for the use of the members of the General Assembly, or be distributed among them, at the public expense.

SECTION 17. No Senator or Delegate, after qualifying as such, notwithstanding he may thereafter resign, shall during the whole period of time, for which he was elected, be eligible to any office, which shall have been created, or the salary, or profits of which shall have been increased, during such term.

SECTION 18. No Senator or Delegate shall be liable in any civil action, or criminal prosecution, whatever, for words spoken in debate.

SECTION 19. Each House shall be judge of the qualifications and elections of its members, as prescribed by the Constitution and Laws of the State, and shall appoint its own officers, determine the rules of its own proceedings, punish a member for disorderly or disrespectful behaviour and with the consent of two-thirds of its whole number of members elected, expel a member; but no member shall be expelled a second time for the same offense.

SECTION 20. A majority of the whole number of members elected to each House shall constitute a quorum for the transaction of business; but a smaller number may adjourn from day to day, and compel the attendance of absent members, in such manner, and under such penalties, as each House may prescribe.

SECTION 21. The doors of each House, and of the Committee of the Whole, shall be open, except when the business is such as ought to be kept secret.

SECTION 22. Each House shall keep a Journal of its proceedings, and cause the same to be published. The yeas and nays of members on any question, shall at the call of any five of them in the House of Delegates, or one in the Senate, be entered on the Journal.

SECTION 23. Each House may punish by imprisonment, during the session of the General Assembly, any person, not a member, for disrespectful, or disorderly behavior in its presence, or for obstructing any of its proceedings, or any of its officers in the execution of their duties; provided, such imprisonment shall not, at any one time, exceed ten days.

SECTION 24. The House of Delegates may inquire, on the oath of witnesses, into all complaints, grievances and offences, as the grand inquest of the State, and may commit any person, for any crime, to the public jail, there to remain, until discharged by due course of Law. They may examine and pass all accounts of the State, relating either to the collection or expenditure of the revenue, and appoint auditors to state and adjust the same. They may call for all public, or official papers and records, and send for persons, whom they may judge necessary in the course of their inquiries, concerning affairs relating to the public interest, and may direct all office bonds which shall be made payable to the State, to be sued for any breach thereof; and with a view to the more certain prevention, or correction of the abuses in the expenditures of the money of the State, the General Assembly shall create, at every session thereof, a Joint Standing Committee of the Senate and House of Delegates, who shall have power to send for persons, and examine them on oath, and call for Public, or Official Papers and Records, and whose duty it shall be to examine and report upon all contracts made for printing stationery, and purchases for the Public offices, and the Library, and all expenditures therein, and upon all matters of alleged abuse in expenditures, to which their attention may be called by Resolution of either House of the General Assembly.

SECTION 25. Neither House shall, without the consent of the other, adjourn for more than three days, at any one time, nor adjourn to any other place, than that in which the House shall be sitting, without the concurrent vote of two-thirds of the members present.

SECTION 26. The House of Delegates shall have the sole power of impeachment in all cases; but a majority of all the members elected must concur in the impeachment. All impeachments shall be tried by the Senate, and when sitting for that purpose, the Senators shall be on oath, or affirmation, to do justice according to the law and evidence; but no person shall be convicted without the concurrence of two-thirds of all the Senators elected.

SECTION 27.

(a) Any bill may originate in either House of the General Assembly and be altered, amended or rejected by the other. No bill shall originate in either House during the last thirty-five calendar days of a regular session, unless two-thirds of the members elected thereto shall so determine by yeas and nays, and in addition the two Houses by joint and similar rule may further regulate the right to introduce bills during this period. A bill may not become a law until it is read on three different days of the session in each House, unless two-thirds of the members elected to the House where such bill is pending determine by yeas and nays, and no bill shall be read a third time until it shall have been actually engrossed or printed for a third reading.

(b) Each House may adopt by rule a "consent calendar" procedure permitting bills to be read and voted upon as a single group on first, second and third readings, provided that the members of each House are afforded reasonable notice of the bills to be placed upon each "consent calendar." Upon the objection of any member, any bill in question shall be removed from the "consent calendar."

SECTION 28. No bill, nor single group of bills placed on the "consent calendar," shall become a Law unless it be passed in each House by a majority of the whole number of members elected, and on its final passage, the yeas and nays be recorded, and on final passage of the bills placed on the "consent calendar" the yeas and nays on the entire group of bills be recorded. A resolution requiring the action of both Houses shall be passed in the same manner.

SECTION 29. The style of all Laws of this State shall be, "Be it enacted by the General Assembly of Maryland:" and all Laws shall be passed by original bill; and every Law enacted by the General Assembly shall embrace but one subject, and that shall be described in its title; and no Law, nor section of Law, shall be revived, or amended by reference to its title, or section only; nor shall any Law be construed by reason of its title, to grant powers, or confer rights which are not expressly contained in the body of the Act; and it shall be the duty of the General Assembly, in amending any article, or section of the Code of Laws of this State, to enact the same, as the said article, or section would read when amended. And whenever the General Assembly shall enact any Public General Law, not amendatory of any section, or article in the said Code, it shall be the duty of the General Assembly to enact the same, in articles and sections, in the same manner, as the Code is arranged, and to provide for the publication of all additions and alterations, which may be made to the said Code.

SECTION 30. Every bill, when passed by the General Assembly, and sealed with the Great Seal, shall be presented by the presiding officer of the House in which it originated to the Governor for his approval. All bills passed during a regular or special session shall be presented to the Governor for his approval no later than 20 days after adjournment. Within 30 days after presentment, if the Governor approves the bill, he shall sign the same in the presence of the presiding officers and Chief Clerks of the Senate and House of Delegates. Every Law shall be recorded in the office of the Court of Appeals, and in due time, be printed, published and certified under the Great Seal, to the several Courts, in the same manner as has been heretofore usual in this State.

SECTION 31. A Law passed by the General Assembly shall take effect the first day of June next after the session at which it may be passed, unless it be otherwise expressly declared therein or provided for in this Constitution.

SECTION 32. No money shall be drawn from the Treasury of the State, by any order or resolution, nor except in accordance with an appropriation by Law; and every such Law shall distinctly specify the sum appropriated, and the object, to which it shall be applied; provided, that nothing herein contained, shall prevent the General Assembly from placing a contingent fund at the disposal of the Executive, who shall report to the General Assembly, at each Session, the amount expended, and the purposes to which it was applied. An accurate statement of the receipts and expenditures of the public money, shall be attached to, and published with the Laws, after each regular Session of the General Assembly.

SECTION 33. The General Assembly shall not pass local, or special Laws, in any of the following enumerated cases, viz.: For extending the time for the collection of taxes; granting divorces; changing the name of any person; providing for the sale of real estate, belonging to minors, or other persons laboring under legal disabilities, by executors, administrators, guardians or trustees; giving effect to informal, or invalid deeds or wills; refunding money paid into the State Treasury, or releasing persons from their debts, or obligations to the State, unless recommended by the Governor, or officers of the Treasury Department. And the General Assembly shall pass no special Law, for any case, for which provision has been made, by an existing General Law. The General Assembly, at its first Session after the adoption of this Constitution, shall pass General Laws, providing for the cases enumerated in this section, which are not already adequately provided for, and for all other cases, where a General Law can be made applicable.

SECTION 34. No debt shall be hereafter contracted by the General Assembly unless such debt shall be authorized by a law providing for the collection of an annual tax or taxes sufficient to pay the interest on such debt as it falls due, and also to discharge the principal thereof within fifteen years from the time of contracting the same; and the taxes laid for this purpose shall not be repealed or applied to any other object until the said debt and interest thereon shall be fully discharged. The annual tax or taxes required to be collected shall not be collected in the event that sufficient funds to pay the principal and interest on the debt are appropriated for this purpose in the annual State budget. The credit of the State shall not in any manner be given, or loaned to, or in aid of any individual association or corporation; nor shall the General Assembly have the power to involve the State in the construction of works of internal improvement which shall involve the faith or credit of the State, except in aid of the construction of works of internal improvement in the counties of St. Mary's, Charles and Calvert, which have had no direct advantage from such works as have been heretofore aided by the State; and provided that such aid, advances or appropriations shall not exceed in the aggregate the sum of five hundred thousand dollars. And they shall not use or appropriate the proceeds of the internal improvement companies, or of the State tax, now levied, or which may hereafter be levied, to pay off the public debt or to any other purpose until the interest and debt are fully paid or the sinking fund shall be equal to the amount of the outstanding debt; but the General Assembly may authorize the Board of Public Works to direct the State Treasurer to borrow in the name of the State, in anticipation of the collection of taxes or other revenues, including proceeds from the sale of bonds, such sum or sums as may be necessary to meet temporary deficiencies in the treasury, to preserve the best interest of the State in the conduct of the various State institutions, departments, bureaus, and agencies during each fiscal year. Subject to the approval of the Board of Public Works and as provided by law, the State Treasurer is authorized to make and sell short-term notes, in the name of the State, in anticipation of the collection of taxes or other revenues, including proceeds from the sale of bonds to meet temporary deficiencies in the Treasury, but such notes must only be made to provide for appropriations already made by the General Assembly. Any revenues anticipated for the purpose of short-term notes, made and sold under the authority of this section, must be so certain as to be readily estimable as to the time of receipt of the revenues and as to the amount of the revenues. The General Assembly may contract debts to any amount that may be necessary for the defense of the State, and provided further that nothing in this section shall be construed to prohibit the raising of funds for the purpose of aiding or compensating in such manner or way as the General Assembly of the State shall deem proper, those citizens of the State who have served, with honor, their Country and State in time of War; provided, however, that such action of the General Assembly shall be effective only when submitted to and approved by a vote of the people of the State at the General Election next following the enactment of such legislation.

SECTION 35. Extra compensation may not be granted or allowed by the General Assembly to any public Officer, Agent, Servant or Contractor, after the service has been rendered, or the contract entered into; nor may the salary or compensation of any public officer be increased or diminished during his term of office except those whose full term of office is fixed by law in excess of 4 years. However, after January 1, 1956, for services rendered after that date, the salary or compensation of any appointed public officer of the Mayor and City Council of Baltimore may be increased or diminished at any time during his term of office; except that as to officers in the Classified City Service, when the salary of any appointed public officer of the Mayor and City Council of Baltimore however, increased or decreased, it may not again be increased or decreased, as the case may be, during the term of such public officer.

SECTION 35A. Nothing in this Constitution shall exempt the salary or compensation of any judge or other public officer from the imposition by the General Assembly of a non-discriminatory tax upon income.

SECTION 36. No Lottery grant shall ever hereafter be authorized by the General Assembly, unless it is a lottery to be operated by and for the benefit of the State.

SECTION 37. Vacant.

SECTION 38. No person shall be imprisoned for debt, but a valid decree of a court of competent jurisdiction or agreement approved by decree of said court for the support of a spouse or dependent children, or for the support of an illegitimate child or children, or for alimony (either common law or as defined by statute), shall not constitute a debt within the meaning of this section.

SECTION 39. The books, papers and accounts of all banks shall be open to inspection under such regulations as may be prescribed by law .

SECTION 40. The General Assembly shall enact no Law authorizing private property to be taken for public use without just compensation, as agreed upon between the parties, or awarded by a jury, being first paid or tendered to the party entitled to such compensation.

SECTION 40A. The General Assembly shall enact no law authorizing private property to be taken for public use without just compensation, to be agreed upon between the parties, or awarded by a jury, being first paid or tendered to the party entitled to such compensation, but where such property is situated in Baltimore City and is desired by this State or by the Mayor and City Council of Baltimore, the General Assembly may provide that such property may be taken immediately upon payment therefor to the owner or owners thereof by the State or by the Mayor and City Council of Baltimore, or into court, such amount as the State or the Mayor and City Council of Baltimore, as the case may be, shall estimate to be the fair value of said property, provided such legislation also requires the payment of any further sum that may subsequently be added by a jury; and further provided that the authority and procedure for the immediate taking of property as it applies to the Mayor and City Council of Baltimore on June 1, 1961, shall remain in force and effect to and including June 1, 1963, and where such property is situated in Baltimore County and is desired by Baltimore County, Maryland, the County Council of Baltimore County, Maryland, may provide for the appointment of an appraiser or appraisers by a Court of Record to value such property and that upon payment of the amount of such evaluation, to the party entitled to compensation, or into Court, and securing the payment of any further sum that may be awarded by a jury, such property may be taken; and where such property is situated in Montgomery County and in the judgment of and upon a finding by the County Council of said County that there is immediate need therefor for right of way for County roads or streets, the County Council may provide that such property may be taken immediately upon payment therefor to the owner or owners thereof, or into court, such amount as a licensed real estate broker or a licensed and certified real estate appraiser appointed by the County Council shall estimate to be the fair market value of such property, provided that the Council shall secure the payment of any further sum that may subsequently be awarded by a jury. In the various municipal corporations within Cecil County, where in the judgment of and upon a finding by the governing body of said municipal corporation that there is immediate need therefor for right of way for municipal roads, streets and extension of municipal water and sewage facilities, the governing body may provide that such property may be taken immediately upon payment therefor to the owner or owners thereof, or into court, such amount as a licensed real estate broker appointed by the particular governing body shall estimate to be a fair market value of such property, provided that the municipal corporation shall secure the payment of any further sum that subsequently may be awarded by a jury. This Section 40A shall not apply in Montgomery County or any of the various municipal corporations within Cecil County, if the property actually to be taken includes a building or buildings.

SECTION 40B. The General Assembly shall enact no law authorizing private property to be taken for public use without just compensation, to be agreed upon between the parties or awarded by a jury, being first paid or tendered to the party entitled to such compensation, except that where such property in the judgment of the State Roads Commission is needed by the State for highway purposes, the General Assembly may provide that such property may be taken immediately upon payment therefor to the owner or owners thereof by said State Roads Commission, or into Court, such amount as said State Roads Commission shall estimate to be of the fair value of said property, provided such legislation also requires the payment of any further sum that may subsequently be awarded by a jury.

SECTION 40C. The General Assembly shall enact no law authorizing private property to be taken for public use without just compensation, to be agreed upon between the parties or awarded by a jury, being first paid or tendered to the party entitled to such compensation, except that where such property, located in Prince George's County in this State, is in the judgment of the Washington Suburban Sanitary Commission needed for water supply, sewerage and drainage systems to be extended or constructed by the said Commission, the General Assembly may provide that such property, except any building or buildings may be taken immediately upon payment therefor by the condemning authority to the owner or owners thereof or into the Court to the use of the person or persons entitled thereto, such amount as the condemning authority shall estimate to be the fair value of said property, provided such legislation requires that the condemning authority's estimate be not less than the appraised value of the property being taken as evaluated by at least one qualified appraiser, whose qualifications have been accepted by a Court of Record of this State, and also requires the payment of any further sum that may subsequently be awarded by a jury, and provided such legislation limits the condemning authority's utilization of the acquisition procedures specified in this section to occasions where it has acquired or is acquiring by purchase or other procedures one-half or more of the several takings of land or interests in land necessary for any given water supply, sewerage or drainage extension or construction project.

SECTION 40D. Vacant.

SECTION 41. Vacant.

SECTION 42. Vacant.

SECTION 43. The property of the wife shall be protected from the debts of her husband.

SECTION 44. Laws shall be passed by the General Assembly, to protect from execution a reasonable amount of the property of the debtor.

SECTION 45. The General Assembly shall provide a simple and uniform system of charges in the offices of Clerks of Courts and Registers of Wills, in the Counties of this State and the City of Baltimore, and for the collection thereof; provided, the amount of compensation to any of the said officers in the various Counties and in the City of Baltimore shall be such as may be prescribed by law.

SECTION 46. The General Assembly shall have power to receive from the United States, any grant, or donation of land, money, or securities for any purpose designated by the United States, and shall administer, or distribute the same according to the conditions of the said grant.

SECTION 47. Vacant.

SECTION 48. Corporations may be formed under general laws, but shall not be created by special act, except for municipal purposes and except in cases where no general laws exist, providing for the creation of corporations of the same general character, as the corporation proposed to be created; and any act of incorporation passed in violation of this section shall be void. All charters granted, or adopted in pursuance of this section, and all charters heretofore granted and created, subject to repeal or modification, may be altered, from time to time, or be repealed; Provided, nothing herein contained shall be construed to extend to Banks, or the incorporation thereof. The General Assembly shall not alter or amend the charter, of any corporation existing at the time of the adoption of this Article, or pass any other general or special law for the benefit of such corporation, except upon the condition that such corporation shall surrender all claim to exemption from taxation or from the repeal or modification of its charter, and that such corporation shall thereafter hold its charter subject to the provisions of this Constitution; and any corporation chartered by this State which shall accept, use, enjoy, or in any wise avail itself of any rights, privileges, or advantages that may hereafter be granted or conferred by any general or special act, shall be conclusively presumed to have thereby surrendered any exemption from taxation to which it may be entitled under its charter, and shall be thereafter subject to taxation as if no such exemption has been granted by its charter.

SECTION 49. The General Assembly shall have power to regulate by Law, not inconsistent with this Constitution, all matters which relate to the Judges of election, time, place and manner of holding elections in this State, and of making returns thereof.

SECTION 50. It shall be the duty of the General Assembly, at its first session, held after the adoption of this Constitution, to provide by Law for the punishment, by fine, or imprisonment in the Penitentiary, or both, in the discretion of the Court, of any person, who shall bribe, or attempt to bribe, any Executive, or Judicial officer of the State of Maryland, or any member, or officer, of the General Assembly of the State of Maryland, or of any Municipal corporation in the State of Maryland, or any Executive officer of such corporation, in order to influence him in the performance of any of his official duties; and, also, to provide by Law for the punishment, by fine, or imprisonment in the Penitentiary, or both, in the discretion of the Court, of any of said officers, or members, who shall demand, or receive any bribe, fee, reward, or testimonial, for the performance of his official duties, or for neglecting, or failing to perform the same; and, also, to provide by Law for compelling any person, so bribing, or attempting to bribe, or so demanding, or receiving a bribe, fee, reward, or testimonial, to testify against any person, or persons, who may have committed any of said offences; provided, that any person, so compelled to testify, shall be exempted from trial and punishment for the offence, of which he may have been guilty; and any person, convicted of such offence, shall, as part of the punishment thereof, be forever disfranchised and disqualified from holding any office of trust, or profit, in this State.

SECTION 51. The personal property of residents of this State, shall be subject to taxation in the County or City where the resident bona fide resides for the greater part of the year for which the tax may or shall be levied, and not elsewhere, except goods and chattels permanently located, which shall be taxed in the City or County where they are so located, but the General Assembly may by law provide for the taxation of mortgages upon property in this State and the debts secured thereby, in the County or City where such property is situated.

SECTION 52.

(1) The General Assembly shall not appropriate any money out of the Treasury except in accordance with the provisions of this section.

(2) Every appropriation bill shall be either a Budget Bill, or a Supplementary Appropriation Bill, as hereinafter provided.

(3) On the third Wednesday in January in each year, (except in the case of a newly elected Governor, and then not later than ten days after the convening of the General Assembly), unless such time shall be extended by the General Assembly, the Governor shall submit to the General Assembly a Budget for the next ensuing fiscal year. Each Budget shall contain a complete plan of proposed expenditures and estimated revenues for said fiscal year and shall show the estimated surplus or deficit of revenues at the end of the preceding fiscal year. Accompanying each Budget shall be a statement showing:

(a) the revenues and expenditures for the preceding fiscal year;

(b) the current assets, liabilities, reserves and surplus or deficit of the State;

(c) the debts and funds of the State;

(d) an estimate of the State's financial condition as of the beginning and end of the preceding fiscal year;

(e) any explanation the Governor may desire to make as to the important features of the Budget and any suggestions as to methods for reduction or increase of the State's revenue.

(4) Each Budget shall embrace an estimate of all appropriations in such form and detail as the Governor shall determine or as may be prescribed by law, as follows:

(a) for the General Assembly as certified to the Governor in the manner hereinafter provided;

(b) for the Executive Department;

(c) for the Judiciary Department, as provided by law, as certified to the Governor;

(d) to pay and discharge the principal and interest of the debt of the State in conformity with Section 34 of Article III of the Constitution, and all laws enacted in pursuance thereof;

(e) for the salaries payable by the State and under the Constitution and laws of the State;

(f) for the establishment and maintenance throughout the State of a thorough and efficient system of public schools in conformity with Article 8 of the Constitution and with the laws of the State; and

(g) for such other purposes as are set forth in the Constitution or laws of the State.

(5) The Governor shall deliver to the presiding officer of each House the Budget and a bill for all the proposed appropriations of the Budget classified and in such form and detail as he shall determine or as may be prescribed by law; and the presiding officer of each House shall promptly cause said bill to be introduced therein, and such bill shall be known as the "Budget Bill." The Governor may, with the consent of the General Assembly, before final action thereon by the General Assembly, amend or supplement said Budget to correct an oversight, provide funds contingent on passage of pending legislation or, in case of an emergency, by delivering such an amendment or supplement to the presiding officers of both Houses; and such amendment or supplement shall thereby become a part of said Budget Bill as an addition to the items of said bill or as a modification of or a substitute for any item of said bill such amendment or supplement may affect.

(5a) The Budget and the Budget Bill as submitted by the Governor to the General Assembly shall have a figure for the total of all proposed appropriations and a figure for the total of all estimated revenues available to pay the appropriations, and the figure for total proposed appropriations shall not exceed the figure for total estimated revenues. Neither the Governor in submitting an amendment or supplement to the Budget Bill nor the General Assembly in amending the Budget Bill shall thereby cause the figure for total proposed appropriations to exceed the figure for total estimated revenues, including any revisions, and in the Budget Bill as enacted the figure for total estimated revenues always shall be equal to or exceed the figure for total appropriations.

(6) The General Assembly shall not amend the Budget Bill so as to affect either the obligations of the State under Section 34 of Article III of the Constitution, or the provisions made by the laws of the State for the establishment and maintenance of a system of public schools or the payment of any salaries required to be paid by the State of Maryland by the Constitution thereof; and the General Assembly may amend the bill by increasing or diminishing the items therein relating to the General Assembly, and by increasing or diminishing the items therein relating to the judiciary, but except as hereinbefore specified, may not alter the said bill except to strike out or reduce items therein, provided, however, that the salary or compensation of any public officer shall not be decreased during his term of office; and such bill, when and as passed by both Houses, shall be a law immediately without further action by the Governor.

(7) The Governor and such representatives of the executive departments, boards, officers and commissions of the State expending or applying for State's moneys, as have been designated by the Governor for this purpose, shall have the right, and when requested by either House of the General Assembly, it shall be their duty to appear and be heard with respect to any Budget Bill during the consideration thereof, and to answer inquiries relative thereto.

(8) Supplementary Appropriation Bill. Either House may consider other appropriations but both Houses shall not finally act upon such appropriations until after the Budget Bill has been finally acted upon by both Houses, and no such other appropriation shall be valid except in accordance with the provisions following:

(a) Every such appropriation shall be embodied in a separate bill limited to some single work, object or purpose therein stated and called herein a Supplementary Appropriation Bill;

(b) Each Supplementary Appropriation Bill shall provide the revenue necessary to pay the appropriation thereby made by a tax, direct or indirect, to be levied and collected as shall be directed in said bill;

(c) No Supplementary Appropriation Bill shall become a law unless it be passed in each House by a vote of a majority of the whole number of the members elected, and the yeas and nays recorded on its final passage;

(d) Each Supplementary Appropriation Bill shall be presented to the Governor of the State as provided in Section 17 of Article 2 of the Constitution and thereafter all the provisions of said section shall apply.

(9) Nothing in this section shall be construed as preventing the General Assembly from passing at any time, in accordance with the provisions of Section 28 of Article 3 of the Constitution and subject to the Governor's power of approval as provided in Section 17 of Article 2 of the Constitution, an appropriation bill to provide for the payment of any obligation of the State within the protection of Section 10 of Article 1 of the Constitution of the United States.

(10) If the Budget Bill shall not have been finally acted upon by the Legislature seven days before the expiration of the regular session, the Governor shall issue a proclamation extending the session for some further period as may, in his judgment, be necessary for the passage of such bill; but no other matter than such bill shall be considered during such extended session except a provision for the cost thereof.

(11) For the purpose of making up the Budget, the Governor shall require from the proper State officials (including all executive departments, all executive and administrative offices, bureaus, boards, commissions and agencies that expend or supervise the expenditure of, and all institutions applying for State moneys and appropriations) such itemized estimates and other information, in such form and at such times as directed by the Governor. An estimate for a program required to be funded by a law which will be in effect during the fiscal year covered by the Budget and which was enacted before July 1 of the fiscal year prior to that date shall provide a level of funding not less than that prescribed in the law. The estimates for the Legislative Department, certified by the presiding officer of each House, of the Judiciary, as provided by law, certified by the Chief Judge of the Court of Appeals, and for the public schools, as provided by law, shall be transmitted to the Governor, in such form and at such times as directed by the Governor, and shall be included in the Budget without revision.

(12) The Governor may provide for public hearings on all estimates and may require the attendance at such hearings of representatives of all agencies, and for all institutions applying for State moneys. After such public hearings he may, in his discretion, revise all estimates except those for the legislative and judiciary departments, and for the public schools, as provided by law, and except that he may not reduce an estimate for a program below a level of funding prescribed by a law which will be in effect during the fiscal year covered by the Budget, and which was enacted before July 1 of the fiscal year prior thereto.

(13) The General Assembly may, from time to time, enact such laws not inconsistent with this section, as may be necessary and proper to carry out its provisions.

(14) In the event of any inconsistency between any of the provisions of this Section and any of the other provisions of the Constitution, the provisions of this Section shall prevail. But nothing herein shall in any manner affect the provisions of Section 34 of Article 3 of the Constitution or of any laws heretofore or hereafter passed in pursuance thereof, or be construed as preventing the Governor from calling extraordinary sessions of the General Assembly, as provided by Section 16 of Article 2, or as preventing the General Assembly at such extraordinary sessions from considering any emergency appropriation or appropriations.

(15) If any item of any appropriation bill passed under the provisions of this Section shall be held invalid upon any ground, such invalidity shall not affect the legality of the bill or of any other item of such bill or bills.

SECTION 53.

(a) There is a Transportation Trust Fund.

(b) Except as provided in subsection (e) of this section, the funds in the Transportation Trust Fund may be used only:

(1) For the purpose of paying the principal of and interest on transportation bonds as they become due and payable; and

(2) After meeting debt service requirements for transportation bonds, for any lawful purpose related to the construction and maintenance of an adequate highway system in the State or any other purpose related to transportation.

(c) Except as provided in subsection (e) of this section, funds in the Transportation Trust Tund may not be transferred to the General Fund or a special fund of the State.

(d) This section does not apply to:

(1) An allocation or use of highway user revenues for the counties, municipalities, or Baltimore City that is authorized under Title 8, Subtitle 4 of the Transportation Article; or

(2) A transfer of funds in the Transportation Trust Fund to the Maryland Transportation Authority or the Maryland Transportation Authority Fund.

(e) Funds in the Transportation Trust Fund may be used for a purpose not related to transportation or transferred to the General Fund or a special fund of the State if:

(1) The Governor, by executive order, declares a fiscal emergency exists; and

(2) The General Assembly, by legislation passed on a yea and nay vote supported by three-fifths of all the members elected to each of the two houses of the General Assembly, concurs with the use or transfer of the funds.

SECTION 54. No County of this State shall contract any debt, or obligation, in the construction of any Railroad, Canal, or other Work of Internal Improvement, nor give, or loan its credit to, or in aid of any association, or corporation, unless authorized by an Act of the General Assembly.

SECTION 55. The General Assembly shall pass no Law suspending the privilege of the Writ of Habeas Corpus.

SECTION 56. The General Assembly shall have power to pass all such Laws as may be necessary and proper for carrying into execution the powers vested, by this Constitution, in any Department, or office of the Government, and the duties imposed upon them thereby.

SECTION 57. The Legal Rate of Interest shall be Six per cent per annum, unless otherwise provided by the General Assembly.

SECTION 58. The Legislature shall provide by Law for State and municipal taxation upon the revenues accruing from business done in the State by all foreign corporations.

SECTION 59. The Legislature shall pass no law creating the office of "State Pension Commissioner", or establishing any general pension system within this State.

SECTION 60. The General Assembly of Maryland shall have the power to provide by suitable general enactment

(a) for the suspension of sentence by the Court in criminal cases;

(b) for any form of the indeterminate sentence in criminal cases, and

(c) for the release upon parole in whatever manner the General Assembly may prescribe, of convicts imprisoned under sentence for crimes.

SECTION 61.

(a) The General Assembly may authorize and empower any county or any municipal corporation, by public local law:

(1) To carry out urban renewal projects which shall be limited to slum clearance in slum or blighted areas and redevelopment or the rehabilitation of slum or blighted areas, and to include the acquisition, within the boundary lines of such county or municipal corporation, of land and property of every kind and any right, interest, franchise, easement or privilege therein, by purchase, lease, gift, condemnation or any other legal means. The term "slum area" shall mean any area where dwellings predominate which, by reason of depreciation, overcrowding, faulty arrangement or design, lack of ventilation, light or sanitary facilities, or any combination of these factors, are detrimental to the public safety, health or morals. The term "blighted area" shall mean an area in which a majority of buildings have declined in productivity by reason of obsolescence, depreciation or other causes to an extent they no longer justify fundamental repairs and adequate maintenance.

(2) To sell, lease, convey, transfer or otherwise dispose of any of said land or property, regardless of whether or not it has been developed, redeveloped, altered or improved and irrespective of the manner or means in or by which it may have been acquired, to any private, public or quasi public corporation, partnership, association, person or other legal entity.

No land or property taken by any county or any municipal corporation for any of the aforementioned purposes or in connection with the exercise of any of the powers which may be granted to such county or municipal corporation pursuant to this section by exercising the power of eminent domain shall be taken without just compensation, as agreed upon between the parties, or awarded by a jury, being first paid or tendered to the party entitled to such compensation.

All land or property needed, or taken by the exercise of the power of eminent domain, by any county or any municipal corporation for any of the aforementioned purposes or in connection with the exercise of any of the powers which may be granted pursuant to this Section is hereby declared to be needed or taken for public uses and purposes. Any or all of the activities authorized pursuant to this section shall constitute governmental functions undertaken for public uses and purposes and the power of taxation may be exercised, public funds expended and public credit extended in furtherance thereof.

(b) The General Assembly may grant to any county or any municipal corporation, by public local law, any and all additional power and authority necessary or proper to carry into full force and effect any and all of the specific powers authorized by this section and to fully accomplish any and all of the purposes and objects contemplated by the provisions of this section, provided such additional power or authority is not inconsistent with the terms and provisions of this section or with any other provision or provisions of the Constitution of Maryland.

(c) The General Assembly of Maryland, by public local law, may establish or authorize the establishment of a public body or agency to undertake in a county or municipal corporation (other than Baltimore City) the activities authorized by this section, and may provide that any or all of the powers, except the power of taxation, herein authorized to be granted to such county or municipal corporation shall be vested in such public body or agency or in any existing public body or agency.

(d) The General Assembly may place such other and further restrictions or limitations on the exercise of any of the powers provided for in this section, as it may deem proper and expedient.

(e) The provisions of this section are independent of, and shall in no way affect, the powers granted under Article XIB of the Constitution of Maryland, title "City of Baltimore - Land Development and Redevelopment." Also, the power provided in this section for the General Assembly to enact public local laws authorizing any municipal corporation or any county to carry out urban renewal projects prevails over the restrictions contained in Article XIA "Local Legislation" and in Article XIE "Municipal Corporations" of this Constitution.

ARTICLE IV: JUDICIARY DEPARTMENT

Part I - General Provisions:

SECTION 1. The Judicial power of this State is vested in a Court of Appeals, such intermediate courts of appeal as the General Assembly may create by law, Circuit Courts, Orphans' Courts, and a District Court. These Courts shall be Courts of Record, and each shall have a seal to be used in the authentication of all process issuing from it.

SECTION 1A. The several Courts existing in this State at the time of the adoption of this Constitution shall, until superseded under its provisions, continue with like powers and jurisdiction, and in the exercise thereof, both at Law and in Equity, in all respects, as if this Constitution had not been adopted; and when said Courts shall be so superseded, all causes, then depending in said Courts, shall pass into the jurisdiction of the several Courts, by which they may, respectively, be superseded.

SECTION 2. The Judges of all of the said Courts shall be citizens of the State of Maryland, and qualified voters under this Constitution, and shall have resided therein not less than five years, and not less than six months next preceding their election, or appointment, as the case may be, in the city, county, district, judicial circuit, intermediate appellate judicial circuit or appellate judicial circuit for which they may be, respectively, elected, or appointed. They shall be not less than thirty years of age at the time of their election or appointment, and shall be selected from those who have been admitted to practice law in this State, and who are most distinguished for integrity, wisdom and sound legal knowledge.

SECTION 3. Except for Judges of the District Court, the Judges of the several Courts other than the Court of Appeals or any intermediate courts of appeal shall, subject to the provisions of Section 5 of this Article of the Constitution, be elected in Baltimore City and in each county, by the qualified voters of the city and of each county, respectively, all of the said Judges to be elected at the general election to be held on the Tuesday after the first Monday in November, as now provided for in the Constitution. Each of the said Judges shall hold his office for the term of fifteen years from the time of his election, and until his successor is elected and qualified, or until he shall have attained the age of seventy years, whichever may first happen, and be re-eligible thereto until he shall have attained the age of seventy years, and not after. In case of the inability of any of said Judges to discharge his duties with efficiency, by reason of continued sickness, or of physical or mental infirmity, it shall be in the power of the General Assembly, two-thirds of the members of each House concurring, with the approval of the Governor to retire said Judge from office.

SECTION 3A.

(a) (1) Except as provided in paragraph (2) of this subsection, any former judge, except a former judge of the Orphans' Court, may be assigned by the Chief Judge of the Court of Appeals, upon approval of a majority of the court, to sit temporarily in any court of this State, except an Orphans' Court, as provided by law.

(2)(i) a retired judge of the Circuit Court for Montgomery County that sits as the Orphans' Court for Montgomery County may be assigned by the Chief Judge of the Court of Appeals, upon approval of a majority of the Court of Appeals, to do an act that a judge of the Orphans' Court for Montgomery County is authorized to perform.

(ii) a retired judge of the Circuit Court for Harford County that sits as the Orphans' Court for Harford County may be assigned by the Chief Judge of the Court of Appeals, upon approval of a majority of the Court of Appeals, to do an act that a judge of the Orphans' Court for Harford County is authorized to perform.

(b) The provisions of this section apply, not withstanding provisions appearing elsewhere in this Article pertaining to retirement of judges upon attaining age 70.

SECTION 4. Any Judge shall be removed from office by the Governor, on conviction in a Court of Law, of incompetency, of wilful neglect of duty, misbehavior in office, or any other crime, or on impeachment, according to this Constitution, or the Laws of the State; or on the address of the General Assembly, two-thirds of each House concurring in such address, and the accused having been notified of the charges against him, and having had opportunity of making his defence.

SECTION 4A.

(a) There is a Commission on Judicial Disabilities composed of eleven persons appointed by the Governor of Maryland, by and with the advice and consent of the Senate.

(b) The members of the Commission shall be citizens and residents of this State.

(c) (1) Three members of the Commission shall be appointed from among the judges of the State, with one member representing the appellate courts, one member representing the circuit courts, and one member representing the District Court.

(2) Three members shall be appointed from among those persons who are admitted to practice law in the State, who have been so engaged for at least seven years, and who are not judges of any court.

(3) Five members shall represent the public, who may not be active or retired judges, who are not admitted to practice law in this State, and who may not have a financial relationship with or receive compensation from a judge or a person admitted to practice law in this State.

(4) The composition of the Commission should reflect the race, gender, and geographic diversity of the population of the State.

(d) The term of office of each member is four years commencing on January 1 following the expiration of the member's predecessor's term. A member may not serve more than two four-year terms, or for more than a total of ten years if appointed to fill a vacancy.

(e) A member's membership automatically terminates:

(1) When any member of the Commission appointed from among judges in the State ceases to be a judge;

(2) When any member appointed from among those admitted to practice law becomes a judge;

(3) When any member representing the public becomes a judge or is admitted to the practice of law in this State or has a financial relationship with or receives compensation from a judge or a person admitted to practice law in this State; or

(4) When any member ceases to be a resident of the State.

(f) Any vacancies on the Commission shall be filled for the unexpired term by the Governor in the same manner as for making of appointments to the Commission and subject to the same qualifications which were applicable to the person causing the vacancy.

(g) A member of the Commission may not receive any compensation for the member's services as such but shall be allowed any expenses necessarily incurred in the performance of the member's duties as such a member

SECTION 4B.

(a) (1) The Commission on Judicial Disabilities has the power to:

(i) investigate complaints against any judge of the Court of Appeals, any intermediate courts of appeal, the Circuit Courts, the District Court of Maryland, or the Orphans' Court; and

(ii) conduct hearings concerning such complaints, administer oaths and affirmations, issue process to compel the attendance of witnesses and the production of evidence, and require persons to testify and produce evidence by granting them immunity from prosecution or from penalty or forfeiture.

(2) The Commission has the power to issue a reprimand and the power to recommend to the Court of Appeals the removal, censure or other appropriate disciplining of a judge or, in an appropriate case, retirement.

(3) All proceedings, testimony, and evidence before the Commission shall be confidential and privileged, except as provided by rule of the Court of Appeals; the record and any proceeding filed with the Court of Appeals shall lose its confidential character, except as ordered by the Court of Appeals.

(4) No judge shall participate as a member of the Commission in any proceedings involving that judge's own conduct, and the Governor shall appoint another judge as a substitute member of the Commission for those proceedings.

(5) The Court of Appeals shall prescribe by rule the means to implement and enforce the powers of the Commission and the practice and procedure before the Commission.

(b) (1) Upon any recommendation of the Commission, the Court of Appeals, after a hearing and upon a finding of misconduct while in office, or of persistent failure to perform the duties of the office, or of conduct prejudicial to the proper administration of justice, may remove the judge from office or may censure or otherwise discipline the judge, or the Court of Appeals, after hearing and upon a finding of disability which is or is likely to become permanent and which seriously interferes with the performance of the judge's duties, may retire the judge from office.

(2) A judge removed under this section, and the judge's surviving spouse, shall have the rights and privileges accruing from the judge's judicial service only to the extent prescribed by the order of removal.

(3) A judge retired under this section shall have the rights and privileges prescribed by law for other retired judges.

(4) No judge of the Court of Appeals shall sit in judgment in any hearing involving that judge's own conduct.

(c) This section is alternative to, and cumulative with, the methods of retirement and removal provided in Sections 3 and 4 of this Article, and in Section 26 of Article III of this Constitution.

SECTION 5. Upon every occurrence or recurrence of a vacancy through death, resignation, removal, disqualification by reason of age or otherwise, or expiration of the term of fifteen years of any judge of a circuit court, or creation of the office of any such judge, or in any other way, the Governor shall appoint a person duly qualified to fill said office, who shall hold the same until the election and qualification of his successor. His successor shall be elected at the first biennial general election for Representatives in Congress after the expiration of the term of fifteen years (if the vacancy occurred in that way) or the first such general election after one year after the occurrence of the vacancy in any other way than through expiration of such term. Except in case of reappointment of a judge upon expiration of his term of fifteen years, no person shall be appointed who will become disqualified by reason of age and thereby unable to continue to hold office until the prescribed time when his successor would have been elected.

SECTION 5A.

(a) A vacancy in the office of a judge of an appellate court, whether occasioned by the death, resignation, removal, retirement, disqualification by reason of age, or rejection by the voters of an incumbent, the creation of the office of a judge, or otherwise, shall be filled as provided in this section.

(b) Upon the occurrence of a vacancy the Governor shall appoint, by and with the advice and consent of the Senate, a person duly qualified to fill said office who shall hold the same until the election for continuance in office as provided in subsections (c) and (d).

(c) The continuance in office of a judge of the Court of Appeals is subject to approval or rejection by the registered voters of the appellate judicial circuit from which he was appointed at the next general election following the expiration of one year from the date of the occurrence of the vacancy which he was appointed to fill, and at the general election next occurring every ten years thereafter.

(d) The continuance in office of a judge of the Court of Special Appeals is subject to approval or rejection by the registered voters of the geographical area prescribed by law at the next general election following the expiration of one year from the date of the occurrence of the vacancy which he was appointed to fill, and at the general election next occurring every ten years thereafter.

(e) The approval or rejection by the registered voters of a judge as provided for in subsections (c) and (d) shall be a vote for the judge's retention in office for a term of ten years or his removal. The judge's name shall be on the appropriate ballot, without opposition, and the voters shall vote yes or no for his retention in office. If the voters reject the retention in office of a judge, or if the vote is tied, the office becomes vacant ten days after certification of the election returns.

(f) An appellate court judge shall retire when he attains his seventieth birthday.

(g) A member of the General Assembly who is otherwise qualified for appointment to judicial office is not disqualified by reason of his membership in a General Assembly which proposed or enacted any constitutional amendment or statute affecting the method of selection. Continuance in office, or retirement or removal of a judge, the creation or abolition of a court, an increase or decrease in the number of judges of any court, or an increase or decrease in the salary, pension or other allowances of any judge.

SECTION 6. All Judges shall, by virtue of their offices, be Conservators of the Peace throughout the State; and no fees, or perquisites, commission, or reward of any kind shall be allowed to any Judge in this State, besides his annual salary, for the discharge of any Judicial duty.

SECTION 7. No Judge shall sit in any case wherein he may be interested, or where either of the parties may be connected with him, by affinity or consanguinity, within such degrees as now are, or may hereafter be prescribed by Law, or where he shall have been of counsel in the case.

SECTION 8.

(a) The parties to any cause may submit the same to the Court for determination without the aid of a jury.

(b) In all cases of presentments or indictments for offenses that are punishable by death, on suggestion in writing under oath of either of the parties to the proceedings that the party cannot have a fair and impartial trial in the court in which the proceedings may be pending, the court shall order and direct the record of proceedings in the presentment or indictment to be transmitted to some other court having jurisdiction in such case for trial.

(c) In all other cases of presentment or indictment, and in all suits or actions at law or issues from the Orphans' Court pending in any of the courts of law in this State which have jurisdiction over the cause or case, in addition to the suggestion in writing of either of the parties to the cause or case that the party cannot have a fair and impartial trial in the court in which the cause or case may be pending, it shall be necessary for the party making the suggestion to make it satisfactorily appear to the court that the suggestion is true, or that there is reasonable ground for the same; and thereupon the court shall order and direct the record of the proceedings in the cause or case to be transmitted to some other court, having jurisdiction in the cause or case, for trial. The right of removal also shall exist on suggestion in a cause or case in which all the judges of the court may be disqualified under the provisions of this Constitution to sit. The court to which the record of proceedings in such suit or action, issue, presentment or indictment is transmitted, shall hear and determine that cause or case in the same manner as if it had been originally instituted in that court. The General Assembly shall modify the existing law as may be necessary to regulate and give force to this provision.

SECTION 9. The Judge, or Judges of any Court, may appoint such officers for their respective Courts as may be found necessary. The General Assembly may provide, by Law, for compensation for all such officers; and the said Judge or Judges shall, from time to time, investigate the expenses, costs and charges of their respective courts, with a view to a change or reduction thereof, and report the result of such investigation to the General Assembly for its action.

SECTION 10.

(a) (1) The Clerks of the Courts shall have charge and custody of records and other papers and shall perform all the duties which appertain to their offices, as are regulated by Law.

(2) The office and business of the Clerks, in all their departments, shall be subject to and governed in accordance with rules adopted by the Court of Appeals pursuant to Section 18 of this article.

(b) The offices of the Clerks shall be funded through the State budget. All fees, commissions, or other revenues established by Law for these offices shall be State revenues, unless provided otherwise by the General Assembly.

SECTION 11. The election for Judges, herein before provided, and all elections for Clerks, Registers of Wills, and other officers, provided in this Constitution, except State's Attorneys, shall be certified, and the returns made, by the Clerks of the Circuit Courts of the Counties, and the Clerk of the Superior Court of Baltimore City, respectively, to the Governor, who shall issue commissions to the different persons for the offices to which they shall have been, respectively, elected; and in all such elections for offices other than judges of an appellate court, the person having the greatest number of votes, shall be declared to be elected.

SECTION 12. In case of any contested election for Judges, Clerks of the Courts of Law, and Registers of Wills, the Governor shall send the returns to the House of Delegates, which shall judge of the election and qualification of the candidates at such election; and if the judgment shall be against the one who has been returned elected, or the one who has been commissioned by the Governor, the House of Delegates shall order a new election within thirty days.

SECTION 13. All Public Commissions and Grants shall run thus: "The State of Maryland, etc.," and shall be signed by the Governor, with the Seal of the State annexed; all writs and process shall run in the same style, and be tested, sealed and signed, as heretofore, or as may hereafter be, provided by Law; and all indictments shall conclude, "against the peace, government and dignity of the State."

SECTION 13A. Vacant.

Part II - Courts of Appeal

SECTION 14. The Court of Appeals shall be composed of seven judges, one from the First Appellate Judicial Circuit consisting of Caroline, Cecil, Dorchester, Kent, Queen Anne's, Somerset, Talbot, Wicomico, and Worcester counties; one from the Second Appellate Judicial Circuit consisting of Baltimore and Harford counties; one from the Third Appellate Judicial Circuit, consisting of Allegany, Carroll, Frederick, Garrett, Howard and Washington counties; one from the Fourth Appellate Judicial Circuit, consisting of Prince George's County; one from the Fifth Appellate Judicial Circuit, consisting of Anne Arundel, Calvert, Charles, and St. Mary's counties; one from the Sixth Appellate Judicial Circuit, consisting of Baltimore City; and one from the Seventh Appellate Judicial Circuit, consisting of Montgomery County. The Judges of the Court of Appeals shall be residents of their respective Appellate Judicial Circuits. The term of each Judge of the Court of Appeals shall begin on the date of his qualification. One of the Judges of the Court of Appeals shall be designated by the Governor as the Chief Judge. The jurisdiction of the Court of Appeals shall be co-extensive with the limits of the State and such as now is or may hereafter be prescribed by law. It shall hold its sessions in the City of Annapolis at such time or times as it shall from time to time by rule prescribe. Its session or sessions shall continue not less than ten months in each year, if the business before it shall so require, and it shall be competent for the judges temporarily to transfer their sittings elsewhere upon sufficient cause. The salary of each Judge of the Court of Appeals shall be that now or hereafter prescribed by the General Assembly and shall not be diminished during his continuance in office. Five of the judges shall constitute a quorum, and five judges shall sit in each case unless the Court shall direct that an additional judge or judges sit for any case. The concurrence of a majority of those sitting shall be sufficient for the decision of any cause, and an equal division of those sitting in a case has the effect of affirming the decision appealed from if there is no application for reargument as hereinafter provided. In any case where there is an equal division or a three to two division of the Court a reargument before the full Court of seven judges shall be granted to the losing party upon application as a matter of right.

SECTION 14A. The General Assembly may by law create such intermediate courts of appeal as may be necessary. The General Assembly may prescribe the intermediate appellate jurisdiction of these courts of appeal, and all other powers necessary for the operation of such courts.

SECTION 14B. No member of the General Assembly at which the addition of Section 14A was proposed, if otherwise qualified, shall be ineligible for appointment or election as a judge of any intermediate court of appeal, established by law by the General Assembly pursuant to said Section 14A, by reason of his membership in such General Assembly.

SECTION 15. Any judge of the Court of Appeals or of an intermediate court of appeal who heard the cause below either as a trial judge or as a judge of any intermediate court of appeal as the case may be, shall not participate in the decision. In every case an opinion, in writing, shall be filed within three months after the argument or submission of the cause; and the judgment of the Court of Appeals shall be final and conclusive.

SECTION 16. Provision shall be made by Law for publishing Reports of all causes, argued and determined in the Court of Appeals and in the intermediate courts of appeal, which the judges thereof, respectively, shall designate as proper for publication.

SECTION 17. There shall be a Clerk of the Court of Appeals, who shall be appointed by and shall hold his office at the pleasure of said Court of Appeals.

SECTION 18.

(a) The Court of Appeals from time to time shall adopt rules and regulations concerning the practice and procedure in and the administration of the appellate courts and in the other courts of this State, which shall have the force of law until rescinded, changed or modified by the Court of Appeals or otherwise by law. The power of courts other than the Court of Appeals to make rules of practice and procedure, or administrative rules, shall be subject to the rules and regulations adopted by the Court of Appeals or otherwise by law.

(b) (1) The Chief Judge of the Court of Appeals shall be the administrative head of the Judicial system of the State. The Chief Judge of the Court of Appeals shall from time to time require, from each of the judges of the Circuit Courts, of the District Court and of any intermediate courts of appeal, reports as to the judicial work and business of each of the judges and their respective courts.

(2) Subject to paragraphs (3) and (4) of this subsection, the Chief Judge of the Court of Appeals may, in case of a vacancy, or of the illness, disqualification or other absence of a judge or for the purpose of relieving an accumulation of business in any court assign any judge except a judge of the Orphans' Court to sit temporarily in any court except an Orphans' Court.

(3) a retired judge of the Circuit Court for Montgomery County that sits as the Orphans' Court for Montgomery County may be assigned by the Chief Judge of the Court of Appeals, upon approval of a majority of the Court of Appeals, to do an act that a judge of the Orphans' Court for Montgomery County is authorized to perform.

(4) a retired judge of the Circuit Court for Harford County that sits as the Orphans' Court for Harford County may be assigned by the Chief Judge of the Court of Appeals, upon approval of a majority of the Court of Appeals, to do an act that a judge of the Orphans' Court for Harford County is authorized to perform.

(5) Any judge assigned by the Chief Judge of the Court of Appeals pursuant to this section has all the power and authority pertaining to a judge of the court to which the judge is so assigned; and the judge's power and authority shall continue with respect to all cases (including any motion, or other matters incidental thereto) which may come before the judge by virtue of such assignment until the judge's action thereon shall be completed. In the absence of the Chief Judge of the Court of Appeals, the provisions of this section shall be applicable to the senior judge present in the Court of Appeals. The powers of the Chief Judge set forth in this section shall be subject to any rule or regulation adopted by the Court of Appeals.

SECTION 18A. Vacant.

Part IIA - Interim Provisions

SECTION 18B.

(a) For the purpose of implementing the amendments to this article, dealing with the selection and tenure of appellate court judges, the following provisions shall govern.

(b) Each judge of an appellate court who is in office for an elected term on the effective date of these amendments, unless he dies, resigns, retires, or is otherwise lawfully removed, shall continue in office until the general election next after the end of his elected term, or until his seventieth birthday, whichever first occurs. His continuance in office is then subject to the provisions of section 5A (c) and (d) of this article, applicable to judges of that court, but in no event shall any judge continue in office after his seventieth birthday.

(c) Each judge of a court specified in subsection (b) who is in office on the effective date of these amendments, but who has not been elected to that office by the voters, shall, within fifteen days after the effective date of these amendments, be reappointed to that office. His continuance in office is then subject to the provisions of section 5A (c) and (d) of this article, applicable to judges of that court, but in no event shall any judge continue in office after his seventieth birthday.

Part III - Circuit Courts

SECTION 19. The State shall be divided into eight Judicial Circuits, in manner following, viz.: The Counties of Worcester, Wicomico, Somerset, and Dorchester, shall constitute the First Circuit; the Counties of Caroline, Talbot, Queen Anne's, Kent and Cecil, the Second; the Counties of Baltimore and Harford, the Third; the Counties of Allegany, Garrett, and Washington, the Fourth; the Counties of Carroll, Howard and Anne Arundel, the Fifth; the Counties of Montgomery and Frederick, the Sixth; the Counties of Prince George's, Charles, Calvert, and St. Mary's, the Seventh; and Baltimore City, the Eighth.

SECTION 20.

(a) There shall be a Circuit Court for each County and for Baltimore City. The Circuit Courts shall have and exercise, in the respective counties, and Baltimore City, all the power, authority and jurisdiction, original and appellate, which the Circuit Courts of the counties exercised on the effective date of these amendments, and the greater or lesser jurisdiction hereafter prescribed by law.

(b) The judges of the Circuit Courts for Montgomery and Harford counties shall each, alternately and in rotation and on schedules to be established by those judges, sit as an Orphans' Court for their County, and shall have and exercise all the power, authority and jurisdiction which the present Orphans' Courts now have and exercise, or which may hereafter be provided by law.

SECTION 21.

(a) Subject to the provisions of subsection (b) the General Assembly shall determine by law the number of judges of the circuit court in each county and circuit. These judges shall be selected in accordance with Sections 3 and 5 of this Article.

(b) There shall be at least four circuit court judges resident in each circuit, and at least one circuit court judge shall be resident in each county. There shall be at least two such judges resident in Anne Arundel County, at least three resident in Baltimore County, at least four resident in Prince George's County, and at least five resident in Montgomery County.

(c) The senior judge in length of service in each circuit shall be the chief judge of the circuit. The other judges shall be associate judges.

(d) Except as otherwise provided by law, one judge shall constitute a quorum for the transaction of any business.

(e) The terms of the circuit courts shall be determined by law.

(f) A person is not ineligible for appointment or election as a judge because he was a member of the General Assembly at a time when the number or salary of judges were increased or decreased.

SECTION 21A. If the amendments to sections 3 and 21 of Article IV proposed by House Bill 972, Senate Bill 390 (1976), and the amendments to those sections proposed by House Bill 1048 (1976) are ratified by the voters at the election in Nov. 1976, the amendments to those sections proposed in House Bill 972, Senate Bill 390 (1976) shall take effect.

SECTION 22. Where any Term is held, or trial conducted by less than three Circuit Judges, upon the decision or determination of any point, or question, by the Court, it shall be competent to the party, against whom the ruling or decision is made, upon motion, to have the point, or question reserved for the consideration of the three Judges of the Circuit, who shall constitute a court in banc for such purpose; and the motion for such reservation shall be entered of record, during the sitting, at which such decision may be made; and the procedure for appeals to the Circuit Court in banc shall be as provided by the Maryland Rules. The decision of the said Court in banc shall be the effective decision in the premises, and conclusive, as against the party at whose motion said points, or questions were reserved; but such decision in banc shall not preclude the right of Appeal by an adverse party who did not seek in banc review, in those cases, civil or criminal, in which appeal to the Court of Special Appeals may be allowed by Law. The right of having questions reserved shall not, however, apply to trials of Appeals from judgments of the District Court, nor to criminal cases below the grade of felony, except when the punishment is confinement in the Penitentiary; and this Section shall be subject to such provisions as may hereafter be made by Law.

SECTION 23. The Judges of the respective Circuit Courts of this State shall render their decisions, in all cases argued before them, or submitted for their judgment, within two months after the same shall have been so argued or submitted.

SECTION 24. The salary of each Chief Judge and of each Associate Judge of the Circuit Court shall not be diminished during his continuance in office.

SECTION 25. There shall be a Clerk of the Circuit Court for each County and Baltimore City, who shall be elected by a plurality of the qualified voters of said County or City, and shall hold this office for four years from the time of his election, and until his successor is elected and qualified, and be re-eligible, subject to be removed for wilful neglect of duty or other misdemeanor in office, on conviction in a Court of Law. In case of a vacancy in the office of Clerk of a Circuit Court, the Judges of that Court may fill the vacancy until the general election for Delegates to the General Assembly, to be held next thereafter, when a successor shall be elected for the term of four years.

SECTION 26. Deputy clerks and other employees of the office of the Clerk shall be appointed and removed according to procedures set by law.

Part IV - Courts of Baltimore City

SECTION 27. Vacant.

SECTION 28. Vacant.

SECTION 29. Vacant.

SECTION 30. Vacant.

SECTION 31. Vacant.

SECTION 31A. Vacant.

SECTION 32. Vacant.

SECTION 33. Vacant.

SECTION 34. Vacant.

SECTION 35. Vacant.

SECTION 36. Vacant.

SECTION 37. Vacant.

SECTION 38. Vacant.

SECTION 39. Vacant.

Part V - Orphans' Court

SECTION 40.

(a) The qualified voters of the several Counties, except Montgomery County and Harford County, shall elect three Judges of the Orphans' Courts of Counties who shall be citizens of the State and residents, for the twelve months preceding, in the County for which they may be elected.

(b) The qualified voters of the City of Baltimore shall elect three Judges of the Orphans' Court for Baltimore City who shall be citizens of the State and residents, for the twelve months preceding, in Baltimore City and who have been admitted to practice law in this State and are members in good standing of the Maryland Bar.

(c) The qualified voters of Prince George's County shall elect three Judges of the Orphans' Court for Prince George's County who shall be citizens of the State and residents, for the twelve months preceding, in Prince George's County and who have been admitted to practice law in this State and are members in good standing of the Maryland Bar.

(d) The qualified voters of Baltimore County shall elect three Judges of the Orphans' Court for Baltimore County who shall be citizens of the State and residents, for the twelve months preceding, in Baltimore County and who have been admitted to practice law in this State and are members in good standing of the Maryland Bar.

(e) The Judges shall have all the powers now vested in the Orphans' Courts of the State, subject to such changes as the Legislature may prescribe.

(f) Each of the Judges shall be paid such compensation as may be regulated by Law, to be paid by the City or Counties, respectively.

(g) In case of a vacancy in the office of Judge of the Orphans' Court, the Governor shall appoint, subject to confirmation or rejection by the Senate, some suitable person to fill the vacancy for the residue of the term.

SECTION 41. There shall be a Register of Wills in each county of the State, and the City of Baltimore, to be elected by the legal and qualified voters of said counties and city, respectively, who shall hold his office for four years from the time of his election and until his successor is elected and qualified; he shall be re-eligible, and subject at all times to removal for willful neglect of duty, or misdemeanor in office in the same manner that the Clerks of the Courts are removable. In the event of any vacancy in the office of the Register of Wills, said vacancy shall be filled by the Judges of the Orphans' Court, in which such vacancy occurs, until the next general election for Delegates to the General Assembly when a Register shall be elected to serve for four years thereafter.

Part VI - District Court

SECTION 41A. The District Court shall have the original jurisdiction prescribed by law. Jurisdiction of the District Court shall be uniform throughout the State; except that in Montgomery County and other counties and the City of Baltimore, the Court may have such jurisdiction over juvenile causes as is provided by law.

SECTION 41B. The District Court shall consist of the number of judges prescribed by law. The State shall be divided by law into districts. Each district shall consist of one county or two or more entire and adjoining counties. The number of judges shall be allocated among the districts by law, and there shall be at least one District Court judge resident in each district. In any district containing more than one county, there shall be at least one District Court judge resident in each county in the district. Functional divisions of the District Court may be established in any district.

SECTION 41C. Each District Court judge shall devote full time to his judicial duties, shall have the qualifications prescribed by Section 2 of this Article, and shall be a resident of the district in which he holds office. The number of judges for any district may be increased or decreased by the General Assembly from time to time, subject to the requirements of Section 41B of this Article, and any vacancy so created shall be filled as provided in Section 41D of this Article.

SECTION 41D. The Governor, by and with the advice and consent of the Senate, shall appoint each judge of the District Court whenever for any reason a vacancy shall exist in the office. All hearings, deliberations, and debate on the confirmation of appointees of the Governor shall be public, and no hearings, deliberations or debate thereon shall be conducted by the Senate or any committee or subcommittee thereof in secret or executive session. Confirmation by the Senate shall be made upon a majority vote of all members of the Senate. A judge appointed by the Governor may take office upon qualification and before confirmation by the Senate, but shall cease to hold office at the close of the regular annual session of the General Assembly next following his appointment or during which he shall have been appointed by the Governor, if the Senate shall not have confirmed his appointment before then. Each judge appointed by the Governor and confirmed by the Senate shall hold the office for a term of ten years or until he shall have attained the age of seventy years whichever may first occur. If the ten year term of a judge shall expire before that judge shall have attained the age of seventy years, that judge shall be reappointed by the Governor, with the Senate's consent, for another ten year term or until he shall have attained the age of seventy years, whichever may first occur. To the extent inconsistent herewith, the provisions of Section 3 and 5 of this Article shall not apply to judges of the District Court.

SECTION 41E. The Chief Judge of the Court of Appeals shall designate one judge of the District Court as Chief Judge of that Court, to serve as Chief Judge at his pleasure. The Chief Judge of the District Court may assign administrative duties to other judges of the District Court and shall perform such other duties in the administration of the District Court as may be prescribed by rule or by law.

SECTION 41F. The Chief Judge of the District Court shall appoint, to serve at his pleasure, a Chief Clerk of that Court. He shall also appoint, to serve at his pleasure, and upon the recommendation of the administrative judge of the district, a chief administrative clerk for each district. The chief clerk shall perform such duties in the administration of the District Court as may be assigned him by the chief judge or as may be prescribed by rule or by law. Each chief administrative clerk shall perform such duties in the administration of the District Court as may be assigned him by the administrative judge of his district or as may be prescribed by rule of law. There shall be in each County a clerk of the District Court whose appointment, term, and compensation shall be prescribed by law. The Chief Judge of the District Court, upon recommendation of the respective administrative judges, shall appoint such deputy clerks, constables, and other officers of the District Court as may be necessary. It shall be the duty of the General Assembly to prescribe by law a fixed compensation for all such officers.

SECTION 41G.

(a)(1) There shall be district court commissioners in the number and with the qualifications and compensation prescribed by law.

(2) Commissioners in a district shall be appointed by and serve at the pleasure of the Administrative Judge of the district, subject to the approval of the Chief Judge of the District Court.

(b) Commissioners may exercise power only with respect to and only as prescribed by law or rule as to:

(1) warrants of arrest, or bail or collateral or other terms of pre-trial release pending hearing; and

(2) issuance of civil interim peace orders and civil interim protective orders within the jurisdiction of the District Court when the Office of the Clerk of the District Court is not open.

SECTION 41H. The salary of a judge of the District Court shall not be reduced during his continuance in office.

SECTION 41-I. For the purpose of implementing the amendments to Articles IV, XV and XVII of this Constitution, establishing the District Court, the following provisions shall govern.

(a) The provisions of Section 41D of this Article shall govern initial vacancies in the office of judge of the District Court. Each full-time judge of the People's Court of Baltimore City, the Municipal Court of Baltimore City, and of the People's Courts of Anne Arundel, Montgomery, Prince George's, Wicomico Counties and Baltimore County who is in office on the effective date of these amendments shall continue in office as a judge of the District Court in his district and county of residence (or in Baltimore City) for the remainder of the term for which he was elected or appointed, and if his term expires prior to January 1, 1971, such judge shall be re-appointed by the Governor, if the Senate consents, in accordance with the provisions of Section 41D of this Article, subject to the Provisions of the Constitution respecting age, removal and retirement;

provided that the term of any such judge of a People's Court who would be ineligible for appointment as a judge of the District Court under this Article shall expire on the effective date of these amendments. Thereafter, retention of any judge who is retained in office pursuant to the preceding provisions of this subsection shall be pursuant to Section 41D of this Article. No People's Court judge, judge of the Housing Court of Baltimore County, or Justice of the Peace shall be appointed or elected or exercise any power or jurisdiction.

(b) Each full-time clerk of a justice of the peace designated as trial magistrate of a People's Court, of the Municipal Court of Baltimore City, and the chief constable of the People's Court of Baltimore City who is in office on the day before the first Monday in July, 1970, shall become a deputy clerk of the District Court on the first Monday in July 1970. The taking effect of the aforegoing amendments shall not of itself affect the tenure, term, status, retirement, or compensation of any person then holding public office, position, or employment in this State, except as provided in the amendments.

(c) All statutory references to justices of the peace designated as trial magistrates, to People's Courts, to the Municipal Court of Baltimore City or to the Housing Court of Baltimore County, shall be deemed to refer to the District Court in the appropriate district, county or Baltimore City, to the extent not inconsistent with this Constitution.

(d) No member of the General Assembly at which these amendments were proposed, or at which the number of or salary of any such judges may have been increased or decreased by the General Assembly from time to time, if otherwise qualified, is ineligible for appointment or election as a judge of the District Court by reason of his membership in the General Assembly.

SECTION 42. Vacant.

SECTION 43. Vacant.

Part VII – Sheriffs

SECTION 44. There shall be elected in each county and in Baltimore City one person, resident in said county or City, above the age of twenty-five years and for at least five years preceding his election a citizen of the State, to the office of Sheriff. He shall hold office for four years, until his successor is duly elected and qualified, give such bond, exercise such powers and perform such duties as now are or may hereafter be fixed by law.

In case of vacancy by death, resignation, refusal to serve, or neglect to qualify or give bond, or by disqualification or removal from the County or City, the Governor shall appoint a person to be Sheriff for the remainder of the official term. The Sheriff in each county and in Baltimore City shall receive such salary or compensation and such expenses necessary to the conduct of his office as may be fixed by law. All fees collected by the Sheriff shall be accounted for and paid to the Treasury of the several counties and of Baltimore City, respectively.

SECTION 45. Notaries Public may be appointed for each county and the city of Baltimore, in the manner, for the purpose, and with the powers now fixed, or which may hereafter be prescribed by Law.

ARTICLE V: ATTORNEY-GENERAL AND STATE'S ATTORNEYS

Attorney-General

SECTION 1. There shall be an Attorney-General elected by the qualified voters of the State, on general ticket, on the Tuesday next after the first Monday in the month of November, nineteen hundred and fifty-eight, and on the same day, in every fourth year thereafter, who shall hold his office for four years from the time of his election and qualification, and until his successor is elected and qualified, and shall be re-eligible thereto, and shall be subject to removal for incompetency, willful neglect of duty or misdemeanor in office, on conviction in a Court of Law.

SECTION 2. All elections for Attorney-General shall be certified to, and returns made thereof by the Clerks of the Circuit Courts for the several counties, and the Clerk of the Superior Court of Baltimore City, to the Governor of the State, whose duty it shall be to decide on the election and qualification of the person returned; and in case of a tie between two or more persons, to designate which of said persons shall qualify as Attorney-General, and to administer the oath of office to the person elected.

SECTION 3.

(a) The Attorney General shall:

(1) Prosecute and defend on the part of the State all cases pending in the Appellate Courts of the State, in the Supreme Court of the United States or the inferior Federal Courts, by or against the State, or in which the State may be interested, except those criminal appeals otherwise prescribed by the General Assembly.

(2) Investigate, commence, and prosecute or defend any civil or criminal suit or action or category of such suits or actions in any of the Federal Courts or in any Court of this State, or before administrative agencies and quasi legislative bodies, on the part of the State or in which the State may be interested, which the General Assembly by law or joint resolution, or the Governor, shall have directed or shall direct to be investigated, commenced and prosecuted or defended.

(3) When required by the General Assembly by law or joint resolution, or by the Governor, aid any State's Attorney or other authorized prosecuting officer in investigating, commencing, and prosecuting any criminal suit or action or category of such suits or actions brought by the State in any Court of this State.

(4) Give his opinion in writing whenever required by the General Assembly or either branch thereof, the Governor, the Comptroller, the Treasurer or any State's Attorney on any legal matter or subject.

(b) The Attorney General shall have and perform any other duties and possess any other powers, and appoint the number of deputies or assistants, as the General Assembly from time to time may prescribe by law.

(c) The Attorney General shall receive for his services the annual salary as the General Assembly from time to time may prescribe by law, but he may not receive any fees, perquisites or rewards whatever, in addition to his salary, for the performance of any official duty.

(d) The Governor may not employ any additional counsel, in any case whatever, unless authorized by the General Assembly.

SECTION 4. No person shall be eligible to the office of Attorney General, who is not a citizen of this State, and a qualified voter therein, and has not resided and practiced Law in this State for at least ten years.

SECTION 5. In case of vacancy in the office of Attorney General, occasioned by death, resignation, removal from the State, or from office, or other disqualification, the Governor shall appoint a person to fill the vacancy for the residue of the term.

SECTION 6. It shall be the duty of the Clerk of the Court of Appeals and the Clerks of any intermediate courts of appeal, respectively, whenever a case shall be brought into said Courts, in which the State is a party or has interest, immediately to notify the Attorney General thereof.

The State's Attorneys

SECTION 7. There shall be an Attorney for the State in each county and the City of Baltimore, to be styled "The State's Attorney", who shall be elected by the voters thereof, respectively, and shall hold his office for four years from the first Monday in January next ensuing his election, and until his successor shall be elected and qualified; and shall be re-eligible thereto, and be subject to removal therefrom, for incompetency, willful neglect of duty, or misdemeanor in office, on conviction in a Court of Law, or by a vote of two-thirds of the Senate, on the recommendation of the Attorney-General.

SECTION 8. All elections for the State's Attorney shall be certified to, and returns made thereof, by the Clerks of the said Counties and City, to the Judges thereof, having criminal jurisdiction, respectively, whose duty it shall be to decide upon the elections and qualifications of the persons returned; and, in case of a tie between two or more persons, to designate which of said persons shall qualify as State's Attorney, and to administer the oaths of office to the person elected.

SECTION 9. The State's Attorney shall perform such duties and receive such salary as shall be prescribed by the General Assembly. If any State's Attorney shall receive any other fee or reward than such as is or may be allowed by law, he shall, on conviction thereof, be removed from office; provided, that the State's Attorney for Baltimore City shall have the power to appoint a Deputy and such other Assistants as the Supreme Bench of Baltimore City may authorize or approve and until otherwise provided by the General Assembly, the said State's Attorney, Deputy and

Assistants shall receive the following annual salaries: State's Attorney, seven thousand five hundred dollars; Deputy State's Attorney, five thousand dollars; Assistant State's Attorneys, four thousand dollars each; said salaries, or such salaries as the General Assembly may subsequently provide and such expenses for conducting the office of the State's Attorney as the Supreme Bench of Baltimore City may authorize or approve shall be paid by the Mayor and City Council of Baltimore to the extent that the total of them exceeds the fees of his office, or as the General Assembly shall otherwise provide, and the Mayor and City Council of Baltimore shall not be liable for appearance fees to the State's Attorney.

SECTION 10. No person shall be eligible to the office of State's Attorney, who has not been admitted to practice Law in this State, and who has not resided, for at least two years, in the county, or city, in which he may be elected.

SECTION 11. In case of a vacancy in the office of State's Attorney, or of his removal from the county or city in which he shall have been elected, or on his conviction as herein specified, the Judge or Judges resident in the county or, if there be no resident Judge, the Judge or Judges having jurisdiction in the Circuit Court of the county in which the vacancy occurs, or by the Supreme Bench of Baltimore City for a vacancy occurring in Baltimore City, shall appoint a person to fill the vacancy for the residue of the term.

SECTION 12. The State's Attorney in each county, and the City of Baltimore, shall have authority to collect, and give receipt, in the name of the State, for such sums of money as may be collected by him, and forthwith make return of and pay over the same to the proper accounting officer. And the State's Attorney of each county, and the City of Baltimore, before he shall enter on the discharge of his duties, and from time to time thereafter, shall give such corporate surety bond as may hereafter be prescribed by Act of the General Assembly.

ARTICLE VI: TREASURY DEPARTMENT

SECTION 1. There shall be a Treasury Department, consisting of a Comptroller chosen by the qualified electors of the State, who shall receive such salary as may be fixed by law; and a Treasurer, to be appointed on joint ballot by the two Houses of the Legislature at each regular session in which begins the term of the Governor, who shall receive such salary as may be fixed by law. The terms of office of the Comptroller and Treasurer shall be for four years, and until their successors shall qualify; and neither of the officers shall be allowed, or receive any fees, commissions or perquisites of any kind in addition to his salary for the performance of any duty or services whatsoever. In case of a vacancy in the office of the Comptroller by death or otherwise, the Governor, by and with the advice and consent of the Senate, shall fill such vacancy by appointment, to continue until another election and until the qualification of the successor. In case of a vacancy in the office of the Treasurer by death or otherwise, the Deputy Treasurer shall act as Treasurer until the next regular or extraordinary session of the Legislature following the creation of the vacancy, whereupon the Legislature shall choose a successor to serve for the duration of the unexpired term of office. The Comptroller and the Treasurer shall keep their offices at the seat of government, and shall take such oaths and enter into such bonds for the faithful discharge of their duties as are now or may hereafter be prescribed by law.

SECTION 2. The Comptroller shall have the general superintendence of the fiscal affairs of the State; he shall digest and prepare plans for the improvement and management of the revenue, and for the support of the public credit; prepare and report estimates of the revenue and expenditures of the State; superintend and enforce the prompt collection of all taxes and revenues; adjust and settle, on terms prescribed by law, with delinquent collectors and receivers of taxes and State revenue; preserve all public accounts; and decide on the forms of keeping and stating accounts. He, or such of his deputies as may be authorized to do so by the Legislature, shall grant, under regulations prescribed by Law, all warrants for money to be paid out of the Treasury, in pursuance of appropriations by law, and countersign all checks drawn by the Treasurer upon any bank or banks in which the moneys of the State, may, from time to time, be deposited. He shall prescribe the formalities of the transfer of stock, or other evidence of the State debt, and countersign the same, without which such evidence shall not be valid; he shall make to the General Assembly full reports of all his proceedings, and of the state of the Treasury Department within ten days after the commencement of each session; and perform such other duties as shall be prescribed by law.

SECTION 3. The Treasurer shall receive the moneys of the State, and, until otherwise prescribed by law, deposit them, as soon as received, to the credit of the State, in such bank or banks as he may, from time to time, with the approval of the Governor, select (the said bank or banks giving security, satisfactory to the Governor, for the safekeeping and forthcoming, when required of said deposits), and he or such of his deputies as may be authorized to do so by the

Legislature shall disburse the same for the purposes of the State according to law, upon warrants drawn by the Comptroller, or his duly authorized deputy, and on checks countersigned by the Comptroller, or his duly authorized deputy. The Legislature may prescribe, by law, for the Treasurer to disburse the moneys of the State, by a system other than by the use of checks. The Treasurer or such of his deputies as may be authorized to do so by the Legislature shall take receipts for all moneys paid from the Treasury Department; and receipt for moneys received by him shall be endorsed upon warrants signed, by the Comptroller, or such deputy as may be authorized to do so by law, without which warrants, so signed, no acknowledgment of money received into the Treasury shall be valid; and upon warrants issued by the Comptroller, or his duly authorized deputy, the Treasurer shall make arrangements for the payment of the interest of the public debt, and for the purchase thereof, on account of the sinking fund. Every bond, certificate, or other evidence of the debt of the State shall be signed by the Treasurer, Chief Deputy Treasurer, or a Deputy Treasurer, and countersigned by the Comptroller, Chief Deputy Comptroller, or a Deputy Comptroller; and no new certificate or other evidence intended to replace another shall be issued until the old one shall be delivered to the Treasurer, and authority executed in due form for the transfer of the same filed in his office, and the transfer accordingly made on the books thereof, and the certificate or other evidence cancelled; but the Legislature may make provisions for the loss of certificates, or other evidences of the debt; and may prescribe, by law, the manner in which the Treasurer shall receive and keep the moneys of the State.

SECTION 4. The Treasurer shall render his Accounts, quarterly, to the Comptroller; and shall publish, monthly, in such newspapers as the Governor may direct, an abstract thereof, showing the amount of cash on hand, and the place, or places of deposit thereof; and on the third day of each regular session of the Legislature, he shall submit to the Senate and House of Delegates fair and accurate copies of all Accounts by him, from time to time, rendered and settled with the Comptroller. He shall, at all times, submit to the Comptroller the inspection of the money in his hands, and perform all other duties that shall be prescribed by Law.

SECTION 5. The Comptroller shall qualify, and enter on the duties of his office, on the third Monday of January next succeeding the time of his election, or as soon thereafter as practicable. And the Treasurer shall qualify within one month after his appointment by the Legislature.

SECTION 6. Whenever during the recess of the Legislature charges shall be preferred to the Governor against the Comptroller or Treasurer, for incompetency, malfeasance in office, willful neglect of duty, or misappropriation of the funds of the State, it shall be the duty of the Governor forthwith to notify the party so charged, and fix a day for a hearing of said charges; and if, in the case of the Comptroller, from the evidence taken, under oath, on said hearing before the Governor, the said allegations shall be sustained, it shall be the duty of the Governor to remove the Comptroller and appoint another in his place, who shall hold the office for the unexpired term of the Comptroller so removed. However, if, in the case of the Treasurer, from the evidence taken under oath in the hearing before the Governor, the allegations are sustained, it is the duty of the

Governor to remove the Treasurer, and the Deputy Treasurer shall act as Treasurer until the next regular or extraordinary session of the Legislature following the appointment, whereupon a successor shall be chosen by the Legislature who shall serve for the unexpired term of the Treasurer so removed.

ARTICLE VII: SUNDRY OFFICERS

SECTION 1. The County Commissioners of each county not governed by Article XI-A of this Constitution may be elected by the voters of commissioner districts established therein, or by the voters of the entire county, or by a combination of these methods of election, as provided by the General Assembly by law.

SECTION 2. The number, compensation, and powers and duties of the County Commissioners of each county not governed by Article XI-A of this Constitution shall be such as now are or may be hereafter prescribed by law.

SECTION 3. Vacant.

SECTION 4. Vacant.

SECTION 5. Vacant.

SECTION 6. Vacant.

ARTICLE VIII: EDUCATION

SECTION 1. The General Assembly, at its First Session after the adoption of this Constitution, shall by Law establish throughout the State a thorough and efficient System of Free Public Schools; and shall provide by taxation, or otherwise, for their maintenance.

SECTION 2. The System of Public Schools, as now constituted, shall remain in force until the end of the said First Session of the General Assembly, and shall then expire; except so far as adopted, or continued by the General Assembly.

SECTION 3. The School Fund of the State shall be kept inviolate, and appropriated only to the purposes of Education.

ARTICLE IX: MILITIA AND MILITARY AFFAIRS

SECTION 1. The General Assembly shall make, from time to time, such provisions for organizing, equipping and disciplining the Militia, as the exigency may require, and pass such Laws to promote Volunteer Militia organizations as may afford them effectual encouragement.

SECTION 2. There shall be an Adjutant-General, appointed by the Governor, by and with the advice and consent of the Senate. He shall hold his office until the appointment and qualification of his successor, or until removed in pursuance of the sentence of a Court Martial. He shall perform such duties, and receive such compensation, or emoluments, as are now, or may be prescribed by Law. He shall discharge the duties of his office at the seat of Government, unless absent, under orders, on duty; and no other officer of the General Staff of the Militia shall receive salary or pay, except when on service, and mustered in with troops.

SECTION 3. Vacant.

ARTICLE X

Vacant.

ARTICLE XI: CITY OF BALTIMORE

SECTION 1. The Inhabitants of the City of Baltimore, qualified by Law to vote in said city for members of the House of Delegates, shall on the fourth Wednesday of October, eighteen hundred and sixty-seven, and on the same day in every fourth year thereafter, elect a person to be Mayor of the City of Baltimore, who shall have such qualifications, receive such compensation, discharge such duties, and have such powers as are now, or may hereafter be prescribed by Law; and the term of whose office shall commence on the first Monday of November succeeding his election, and shall continue for four years, and until his successor shall have qualified; and he shall be ineligible for the term next succeeding that for which he was elected.

SECTION 2. The City Council of Baltimore shall consist of two branches, one of which shall be called the First Branch, and the other the Second Branch, and each shall consist of such number of members, having such qualification, receiving such compensation, performing such duties, possessing such powers, holding such terms of office, and elected in such manner, as are now, or may hereafter be prescribed by Law.

SECTION 3. An election for members of the First and Second Branch of the City Council of Baltimore shall be held in the City of Baltimore on the fourth Wednesday of October, eighteen hundred and sixty-seven, and for members of the First Branch on the same day in every year thereafter; and for members of the Second Branch on the same day in every second year thereafter; and the qualification for electors of the members of the City Council shall be the same as those prescribed for the electors of Mayor.

SECTION 4. The regular sessions of the City Council of Baltimore, (which shall be annual), shall commence on the third Monday of January of each year, and shall not continue more than ninety days, exclusive of Sundays; but the Mayor may convene the City Council in extra session whenever, and as often as it may appear to him that the public good may require, but no called or extra session shall last longer than twenty days, exclusive of Sundays.
SEC. 5. No person, elected and qualified as Mayor, or as a member of the City Council, shall, during the term for which he was elected, hold any other office of profit or trust, created, or to be created, by the Mayor and City Council of Baltimore, or by any Law relating to the Corporation of Baltimore, or hold any employment, or position, the compensation of which shall be paid, directly or indirectly, out of the City Treasury; nor shall any such person be interested, directly or indirectly, in any contract, to which the City is a party; nor shall it be lawful for any person, holding any office, under the City, to be interested, while holding such office, in any contract, to which the City is a party.

SECTION 6. The Mayor shall, on conviction in a Court of Law, of willful neglect of duty, or misbehavior in office, be removed from office by the Governor of the State, and a successor shall thereafter be elected, as in a case of vacancy.

SECTION 7. From and after the adoption of this Constitution, no debt except as hereinafter provided in this section, shall be created by the Mayor and City Council of Baltimore; nor shall the credit of the Mayor and City Council of Baltimore be given, or loaned to, or in aid of any individual, association, or corporation; nor shall the Mayor and City Council of Baltimore have the power to involve the City of Baltimore in the construction of works of internal improvement, nor in granting any aid thereto, which shall involve the faith and credit of the City, nor make any appropriation therefor, unless the debt or credit is authorized by an ordinance of the Mayor and City Council of Baltimore, submitted to the legal voters of the City of Baltimore, at such time and place as may be fixed by the ordinance, and approved by a majority of the votes cast at that time and place. An ordinance for the authorization of debt or credit as aforesaid may not be submitted to the legal voters of Baltimore City unless the proposed creation of debt or extension of credit is either (1) presented to and approved by a majority of the members of the General Assembly representing Baltimore City no later than the 30th day of the regular session of the General Assembly immediately preceding its submission to the voters, or (2) authorized by an Act of the General Assembly. The ordinance shall provide for the discharge of any such debt or credit within the period of 40 years from the time of contracting the same. The Mayor and City Council may, temporarily, borrow any amount of money to meet any deficiency in the City treasury, and may borrow any amount at any time to provide for any emergency arising from the necessity of maintaining the police, or preserving the health, safety and sanitary condition of the City, and may make due and proper arrangements and agreements for the renewal and extension, in whole or in part, of any and all debts and obligations created according to law before the adoption of this Constitution. The General Assembly may, from time to time, fix a limit upon the aggregate amount of bonds and other evidences of indebtedness of the City outstanding at any one time to the same extent as it fixes such a limit upon the indebtedness of the chartered counties.

SECTION 8. All Laws and Ordinances, now in force, applicable to the City of Baltimore, not inconsistent with this Article, shall be, and they are hereby continued until changed in due course of Law.

SECTION 9. The General Assembly may make such changes in this Article, except in Section seventh thereof, as it may deem best; and this Article shall not be so construed, or taken as to make the political corporation of Baltimore independent of, or free from the control, which the General Assembly of Maryland has over all such Corporations in this State.

ARTICLE XI-A: LOCAL LEGISLATION

SECTION 1. On demand of the Mayor of Baltimore and City Council of the City of Baltimore, or on petition bearing the signatures of not less than 20% of the registered voters of said City or any County (Provided, however, that in any case 10,000 signatures shall be sufficient to complete a petition), the Board of Election Supervisors of said City or County shall provide at the next general or congressional election, occurring after such demand or the filing of such petition, for the election of a charter board of eleven registered voters of said City or five registered voters in any such Counties. Nominations for members for said charter board may be made not less than forty days prior to said election by the Mayor of Baltimore and City Council of the City of Baltimore or the County Commissioners of such County, or not less than twenty days prior to said election by petition bearing the signatures written in their own handwriting (and not by their mark) of not less than 5% of the registered voters of the said City of Baltimore or said County; provided, that in any case Two thousand signatures of registered voters shall be sufficient to complete any such nominating petition, and if not more than eleven registered voters of the City of Baltimore or not more than five registered voters in any such County are so nominated their names shall not be printed on the ballot, but said eleven registered voters in the City of Baltimore or five in such County shall constitute said charter board from and after the date of said election. At said election the ballot shall contain the names of said nominees in alphabetical order without any indication of the source of their nomination, and shall also be so arranged as to permit the voter to vote for or against the creation of said charter board, but the vote cast against said creation shall not be held to bar the voter from expressing his choice among the nominees for said board, and if the majority of the votes cast for and against the creation of said charter board shall be against said creation the election of the members of said charter board shall be void; but if such majority shall be in favor of the creation of said charter board, then and in that event the eleven nominees of the City of Baltimore or five nominees in the County receiving the largest number of votes shall constitute the charter board, and said charter board, or a majority thereof, shall prepare within 18 months from the date of said election a charter or form of government for said city or such county and present the same to the Mayor of Baltimore or President of the Board of County Commissioners of such county, who shall publish the same in at least two newspapers of general circulation published in the City of Baltimore or County within thirty days after it shall be reported to him. Such charter shall be submitted to the voters of said City or County at the next general or Congressional election after the report of said charter to said Mayor of Baltimore or President of the Board of County Commissioners; and if a majority of the votes cast for and against the adoption of said charter shall be in favor of such adoption, the said charter from and after the thirtieth day from the date of such election shall become the law of said City or County, subject only to the Constitution and Public General Laws of this State, and any public local laws inconsistent with the provisions of said charter and any former charter of the City of Baltimore or County shall be thereby repealed.

SECTION 1A. The procedure provided in this section for adoption of a charter may be used in any county in lieu of the procedures provided in Section 1 of this Article, and a charter adopted pursuant to this section has the effect of a charter adopted in accordance with the provisions of Section 1. The board of county commissioners of any county at any time may appoint a charter board. Said charter board shall be registered voters and shall consist of an uneven number of members, not fewer than five or more than nine. The board of county commissioners shall appoint a charter board within thirty days after receiving a petition signed by five percent of the registered voters of the county or by ten thousand voters of the county, whichever is the lesser number. If additional charter board members are nominated by petitions signed by three percent of the registered voters of the county or by two thousand registered voters, whichever is the lesser number, delivered to the board of county commissioners within sixty days after the charter board is appointed, the board of county commissioners shall call a special election not less than thirty or more than ninety days after receiving petitions, unless a regular election falls within the designated period. The appointees of the board of county commissioners and those nominated by petitions shall be placed on the ballot in alphabetical order without party designation. The voters may cast votes for, and elect a number of nominees equal to the number of charter board members originally selected by the board of county commissioners, and those so elected are the charter board. The charter board, within 18 months from the date of its appointment, or if there was an election for some of its members, within 18 months from the date of the election, shall present a proposed charter for the county to the board of county commissioners, which shall publish it at least twice in one or more newspapers of general circulation in the county within thirty days after it is presented. The charter shall be submitted to the voters of the county at a special or regular election held not earlier than thirty days or later than ninety days after publication of the charter. If a majority of the votes cast for and against the adoption of the charter are in favor of its adoption, the charter shall become effective as the charter of the county on the thirtieth day after the election or such later date as shall be specified in the charter.

SECTION 2. The General Assembly shall by public general law provide a grant of express powers for such County or Counties as may thereafter form a charter under the provisions of this Article. Such express powers granted to the Counties and the powers heretofore granted to the City of Baltimore, as set forth in Article 4, Section 6, Public Local Laws of Maryland, shall not be enlarged or extended by any charter formed under the provisions of this Article, but such powers may be extended, modified, amended or repealed by the General Assembly.

SECTION 3. Every charter so formed shall provide for an elective legislative body in which shall be vested the law-making power of said City or County. Such legislative body in the City of Baltimore shall be known as the City Council of the City of Baltimore, and in any county shall be known as the County Council of the County. The chief executive officer or County Executive, if any such charter shall provide for the election of such executive officer or County Executive, or the presiding officer of said legislative body, if such charter shall not provide for the election of a chief executive officer or County Executive, shall be known in the City of Baltimore as Mayor of Baltimore, and in any County as the President or Chairman of the County Council of the County, and all references in the Constitution and laws of this State to the Mayor of Baltimore and City Council of the City of Baltimore or to the County Commissioners of the Counties, shall be construed to refer to the Mayor of Baltimore and City Council of the City of Baltimore and to the President or Chairman and County Council herein provided for whenever such construction would be reasonable. From and after the adoption of a charter by the City of Baltimore, or any County of this State, as hereinbefore provided, the Mayor of Baltimore and City Council of the City of Baltimore or the County Council of said County, subject to the Constitution and Public General Laws of this State, shall have full power to enact local laws of said City or County including the power to repeal or amend local laws of said City or County enacted by the General Assembly, upon all matters covered by the express powers granted as above provided, and, as expressly authorized by statute, to provide for the filling of a vacancy in the County Council or in the chief executive officer or County Executive by special election; provided that nothing herein contained shall be construed to authorize or empower the County Council of any County in this State to enact laws or regulations for any incorporated town, village, or municipality in said County, on any matter covered by the powers granted to said town, village, or municipality by the Act incorporating it, or any subsequent Act or Acts amendatory thereto. Provided, however, that the charters for the various Counties shall specify the number of days, not to exceed forty-five, which may but need not be consecutive, that the County Council of the Counties may sit in each year for the purpose of enacting legislation for such Counties, and all legislation shall be enacted at the times so designated for that purpose in the charter, and the title or a summary of all laws and ordinances proposed shall be published once a week for two successive weeks prior to enactment followed by publication once after enactment in at least one newspaper of general circulation in the county, so that the taxpayers and citizens may have notice thereof. The validity of emergency legislation shall not be affected if enacted prior to the completion of advertising thereof. These provisions concerning publication shall not apply to Baltimore City. All such local laws enacted by the Mayor of Baltimore and City Council of the City of Baltimore or the Council of the Counties as hereinbefore provided, shall be subject to the same rules of interpretation as those now applicable to the Public Local Laws of this State, except that in case of any conflict between said local law and any Public General Law now or hereafter enacted the Public General Law shall control.

SECTION 3A. The charter for the government of any county governed by the provisions of this Article may provide for the election of members of the county council by the voters of councilmanic districts therein established, or by the voters of the entire county, or by a combination of these methods of election.

(b) Repealed.

(c) Repealed.

(d) Repealed.

SECTION 4. From and after the adoption of a charter under the provisions of this Article by the City of Baltimore or any County of this State, no public local law shall be enacted by the General Assembly for said City or County on any subject covered by the express powers granted as above provided. Any law so drawn as to apply to two or more of the geographical sub-divisions of this State shall not be deemed a Local Law, within the meaning of this Act. The term "geographical sub-division" herein used shall be taken to mean the City of Baltimore or any of the Counties of this State.

SECTION 5. Amendments to any charter adopted by the City of Baltimore or by any County of this State under the provisions of this Article may be proposed by a resolution of the Mayor of Baltimore and the City Council of the City of Baltimore, or the Council of the County, or by a petition signed by not less than 20% of the registered voters of the City or County, provided, however, that in any case 10,000 signatures shall be sufficient to complete a petition. A petition shall be filed with the Mayor of Baltimore or the President of the County Council. An amendment so proposed shall be submitted to the voters of the City or County at the next general or congressional election occurring after the passage of the resolution or the filing of the petition. If at the election the majority of the votes cast for and against the amendment shall be in favor thereof, the amendment shall be adopted and become a part of the charter of the City or County from and after the thirtieth day after said election. The amendments shall be published by the Mayor of Baltimore or President of the County Council once a week for five successive weeks prior to the election in at least one newspaper published in said City or County.

SECTION 6. The power heretofore conferred upon the General Assembly to prescribe the number, compensation, powers and duties of the County Commissioners in each County, and the power to make changes in Sections 1 to 6 inclusive, Article XI of this Constitution, when expressly granted as hereinbefore provided, are hereby transferred to the voters of each County and the voters of City of Baltimore, respectively, provided that said powers so transferred shall be exercised only by the adoption or amendment of a charter as hereinbefore provided; and provided further that this Article shall not be construed to authorize the exercise of any powers in excess of those conferred by the Legislature upon said Counties or City as this Article sets forth.

SECTION 7. The word "Petition" as used in this Article means one or more sheets written or printed, or partly written and partly printed. There shall be attached to each paper of signatures filed with a petition an affidavit of the person procuring those signatures that the signatures were affixed in his presence and that, based upon the person's best knowledge and belief, every signature on the paper is genuine and bona fide and that the signers are registered voters at the address set opposite or below their names. The General Assembly shall prescribe by law the form of the petition, the manner for verifying its authenticity, and other administrative procedures which facilitate the petition process and which are not in conflict with this Article. The false signing of any name, or the signing of any fictitious name to said petition shall be forgery, and the making of any false affidavit in connection with said petition shall be perjury.

ARTICLE XI-B: CITY OF BALTIMORE - LAND DEVELOPMENT AND REDEVELOPMENT

SECTION 1. The General Assembly of Maryland, by public local law, may authorize and empower the Mayor and City Council of Baltimore:

(a) To acquire, within the boundary lines of Baltimore City, land and property of every kind, and any right, interest, franchise, easement or privilege therein, by purchase, lease, gift, condemnation or any other legal means, for development or redevelopment, including, but not limited to, the comprehensive renovation or rehabilitation thereof; and

(b) To sell, lease, convey, transfer or otherwise dispose of any of said land or property, regardless of whether or not it has been developed, redeveloped, altered or improved and irrespective of the manner or means in or by which it may have been acquired, to any private, public or quasi public corporation, partnership, association, person or other legal entity.

No land or property taken by the Mayor and City Council of Baltimore for any of the aforementioned purposes or in connection with the exercise of any of the powers which may be granted to the Mayor and City Council of Baltimore pursuant to this Article by exercising the power of eminent domain, shall be taken without just compensation, as agreed upon between the parties, or awarded by a jury, being first paid or tendered to the party entitled to such compensation.

All land or property needed, or taken by the exercise of the power of eminent domain, by the Mayor and City Council of Baltimore for any of the aforementioned purposes or in connection with the exercise of any of the powers which may be granted to the Mayor and City Council of Baltimore pursuant to this Article is hereby declared to be needed or taken for a public use.

SECTION 2. The General Assembly of Maryland may grant to the Mayor and City Council of Baltimore any and all additional power and authority necessary or proper to carry into full force and effect any and all of the specific powers which the General Assembly is authorized to grant to the Mayor and City Council of Baltimore pursuant to this Article and to fully accomplish any and all of the purposes and objects contemplated by the provisions of this Article, provided such additional power or authority is not inconsistent with the terms and provisions of this Article or with any other provision or provisions of the Constitution of Maryland. The General Assembly may place such other and further restrictions or limitations on the exercise of any of the powers which it may grant to the Mayor and City Council of Baltimore under the provisions of this Article as it may deem proper and expedient.

SECTION 3. Vacant.

ARTICLE XI-C: OFF-STREET PARKING

SECTION 1. The General Assembly of Maryland, by public local law, may authorize the Mayor and City Council of Baltimore:

(a) Within the City of Baltimore to acquire land and property of every kind, and any right, interest, franchise, easement or privilege therein, by purchase, lease, gift, condemnation or any other legal means, for storing, parking and servicing self-propelled vehicles, provided, that no petroleum products shall be sold or offered for sale at any entrance to or exit from, any land so acquired or at any entrance to, or exit from, any structure erected thereon, when any entrance to, or exit from, any such land or structure faces on a street or highway which is more than 25 feet wide from curb to curb; and

(b) To sell, lease, convey, transfer or otherwise dispose of any of said land or property, regardless of whether or not it has been developed, redeveloped, altered, or improved and irrespective of the manner or means in or by which it may have been acquired, to any private, public or quasi public corporation, partnership, association, person or other legal entity.

No land or property taken by the Mayor and City Council of Baltimore for any of the aforementioned purposes or in connection with the exercise of any of the powers which may be granted to the Mayor and City Council of Baltimore pursuant to this Article by exercising the power of eminent domain, shall be taken without just compensation, as agreed upon between the parties, or awarded by a jury, being first paid or tendered to the party entitled to such compensation.

All land or property needed, or taken by the exercise of the power of eminent domain, by the Mayor and City Council of Baltimore for any of the aforementioned purposes or in connection with the exercise of any of the powers which may be granted to the Mayor and City Council of Baltimore pursuant to this Article is hereby declared to be needed or taken for a public use.

SECTION 2. The General Assembly of Maryland may grant to the Mayor and City Council of Baltimore any and all additional power and authority necessary or proper to carry into full force and effect any and all of the specific powers which the General Assembly is authorized to grant to the Mayor and City Council of Baltimore pursuant to this Article and to fully accomplish any and all of the purposes and objects contemplated by the provisions of this Article, provided such additional power or authority is not inconsistent with the terms and provisions of this Article or with any other provision or provisions of the Constitution of Maryland. The General Assembly may place such other and further restrictions or limitations on the exercise of any of the powers which it may grant to the Mayor and City Council of Baltimore under the provisions of this Article as it may deem proper and expedient.

SECTION 3. In addition to the powers granted and exercised under Sections 1 and 2, the Mayor and City Council of Baltimore may, by ordinance, borrow money to finance the establishment, construction, erection, alteration, expansion, enlarging, improving, equipping, repairing, maintaining, operating, controlling, and regulating of off-street parking facilities owned or to be owned by the Mayor and City Council of Baltimore, and evidence such borrowing by the issuance of revenue bonds, notes or other obligations to be secured by a pledge of the revenues derived from such facilities, and may further pledge revenues collected from parking taxes, parking fees or charges, parking fines or any other revenue derived from the parking of motor vehicles in the City of Baltimore to or for the payment of such revenue bonds, notes or other obligations; and for such purposes the Commissioners of Finance are empowered to maintain a fund consisting of the revenue pledged herein. The bonds, notes or other obligations issued hereunder and the pledge of revenues, taxes, fees, charges or fines provided for herein shall not constitute a general obligation of nor a pledge of the faith and credit or taxing power of the Mayor and City Council of Baltimore and shall not constitute a debt of the Mayor and City Council of Baltimore within the meaning of Section 7 of Article XI of the Constitution of Maryland. The ordinance may prescribe the form and terms of the bonds, notes or other obligations, the time and manner of public or private sale thereof, and the method and terms of payment therefor, and may authorize the Commissioners of Finance by resolution to determine any matters hereinabove recited and to do any and all things necessary or appropriate in connection with the issuance and sale thereof.

ARTICLE XI-D: PORT DEVELOPMENT

SECTION 1. The General Assembly of Maryland, by public local law, may authorize the Mayor and City Council of Baltimore:

(a) To acquire land and property of every kind, and any right, interest, franchise, easement or privilege therein, in adjoining or in the vicinity of the Patapsco River or its tributaries, by purchase, lease, gift, condemnation or any other legal means, for or in connection with extending, developing or improving the harbor or port of Baltimore and its facilities and the highways and approaches thereto; and providing, further, that the Mayor and City Council of Baltimore shall not acquire any such land or property, or any such right, interest, franchise, easement or privilege therein, for any of said purposes, in any of the counties of this State without the prior consent and approval by resolution duly passed after a public hearing, by the governing body of the county in which such land or property, or such right, interest, franchise, easement or privilege therein, is situate; and provided, further, that Anne Arundel County shall retain jurisdiction and power to tax any land so acquired by the Mayor and City Council of Baltimore under the provisions of this Act.

(b) To sell, lease, convey, transfer or otherwise dispose of any of said land or property, regardless of whether or not it is undeveloped or has been developed, redeveloped, altered, or improved and irrespective of the manner or means in or by which it may have been acquired, to any private, public or quasi public corporation, partnership, association, person or other legal entity.
No land or property taken by the Mayor and City Council of

Baltimore for any of the aforementioned purposes or in connection with the exercise of any of the powers which may be granted to the Mayor and City Council of Baltimore pursuant to this Article by exercising the power of eminent domain, shall be taken without just compensation, as agreed upon between the parties, or awarded by a jury, being first paid or tendered to the party entitled to such compensation.

All land or property needed, or taken by the exercise of the power of eminent domain, by the Mayor and City Council of Baltimore for any of the aforementioned purposes or in connection with the exercise of any of the powers which may be granted to the Mayor and City Council of Baltimore pursuant to this Article is hereby declared to be needed or taken for a public use.

SECTION 2. The General Assembly of Maryland may grant to the Mayor and City Council of Baltimore any and all additional power and authority necessary or proper to carry into full force and effect any and all of the specified powers which the General Assembly is authorized to grant to the Mayor and City Council of Baltimore pursuant to this Article and to fully accomplish any and all of the purposes and objects contemplated by the provisions of this Article, provided such additional power or authority is not inconsistent with the terms and provisions of this Article or with any other provision or provisions of the Constitution of Maryland. The General Assembly may place such other and further restrictions or limitations on the exercise of any of the powers which it may grant to the Mayor and City Council of Baltimore under the provisions of this Article as it may deem proper and expedient.

SECTION 3. Provided, however, that no public local law enacted under the provisions and authority of this Article shall be enacted or construed to authorize the Mayor and City Council of Baltimore to exercise or apply any of the powers or authority in this Article enumerated within the territorial limits of Howard County.

ARTICLE XI-E: MUNICIPAL CORPORATIONS

SECTION 1. Except as provided elsewhere in this Article, the General Assembly shall not pass any law relating to the incorporation, organization, government, or affairs of those municipal corporations which are not authorized by Article 11-A of the Constitution to have a charter form of government which will be special or local in its terms or in its effect, but the General Assembly shall act in relation to the incorporation, organization, government, or affairs of any such municipal corporation only by general laws which shall in their terms and in their effect apply alike to all municipal corporations in one or more of the classes provided for in Section 2 of this Article. It shall be the duty of the General Assembly to provide by law the method by which new municipal corporations shall be formed.

SECTION 2. The General Assembly, by law, shall classify all such municipal corporations by grouping them into not more than four classes based on population as determined by the most recent census made under the authority of the United States or the State of Maryland. No more than one such grouping of municipal corporations into four (or fewer) classes shall be in effect at any time, and the enactment of any such grouping of municipal corporations into four (or fewer) classes shall repeal any such grouping of municipal corporations into four (or fewer) classes then in effect. Municipal corporations shall be classified only as provided in this section and not otherwise.

SECTION 3. Any such municipal corporation, now existing or hereafter created, shall have the power and authority,

(a) to amend or repeal an existing charter or local laws relating to the incorporation, organization, government, or affairs of said municipal corporation heretofore enacted by the General Assembly of Maryland, and

(b) to adopt a new charter, and to amend or repeal any charter adopted under the provisions of this Article.

SECTION 4. The adoption of a new charter, the amendment of any charter or local laws, or the repeal of any part of a charter or local laws shall be proposed either by a resolution of the legislative body of any such municipal corporation or by a petition containing the signatures of at least five per cent of the registered voters of a municipal corporation and filed with the legislative body of said municipal corporation. The General Assembly shall amplify the provisions of this section by general law in any manner not inconsistent with this Article.

SECTION 5. Notwithstanding any other provision in this Article, the General Assembly may enact, amend, or repeal local laws placing a maximum limit on the rate at which property taxes may be imposed by any such municipal corporation and regulating the maximum amount of debt which may be incurred by any municipal corporation. However, no such local law shall become effective in regard to a municipal corporation until and unless it shall have been approved at a regular or special municipal election by a majority of the voters of that municipal corporation voting on the question. No such municipal corporation shall levy any type of tax, license fee, franchise tax or fee which was not in effect in such municipal corporation on January 1, 1954, unless it shall receive the express authorization of the General Assembly for such purpose, by a general law which in its terms and its effect applies alike to all municipal corporations in one or more of the classes provided for in Section 2 of this Article. All charter provisions enacted under the authority of Section 3 of this Article shall be subject to any local laws enacted by the General Assembly and approved by the municipal voters under the provisions of this section.

SECTION 6. All charter provisions, or amendments thereto, adopted under the provisions of this Article, shall be subject to all applicable laws enacted by the General Assembly; except that any local laws, or amendments thereto, relating to the incorporation, organization, government, or affairs of any municipal corporation and enacted before this Article becomes effective, shall be subject to any charter provisions, or amendments thereto, adopted under the provisions of this Article. Any local law, or amendments thereto, relating to the incorporation, organization, government, or affairs of any municipal corporation and in effect at the time this Article becomes effective, shall be subject to any applicable State law enacted after this Article becomes effective. All laws enacted by the General Assembly and in effect at the time this Article becomes effective, shall remain in effect until amended or repealed in accordance with the provisions of this Constitution. Nothing in this Article shall be construed to authorize any municipal corporation, by any amendment or addition to its charter, to permit any act which is prohibited by the laws of this State concerning the observance of the Sabbath Day or the manufacture, licensing or sale of alcoholic beverages.

ARTICLE XI-F: HOME RULE FOR CODE COUNTIES

SECTION 1. For the purposes of this Article,

(1) "code county" means a county which is not a charter county under Article 11A of this Constitution and has adopted the optional powers of home rule provided under this Article; and

(2) "public local law" means a law applicable to the incorporation, organization, or government of a code county and contained in the county's code of public local laws; but this latter term specifically does not include

(i) the charters of municipal corporations under Article 11E of this Constitution,

(ii) the laws or charters of counties under Article 11A of this Constitution,

(iii) laws, whether or not Statewide in application, in the code of public general laws,

(iv) laws which apply to more than one county, and

(v) ordinances and resolutions of the county government enacted under public local laws.

SECTION 2. The governing body of any county, by a vote of at least two-thirds of the members elected thereto, may propose by resolution that the county become a code county and be governed by the provisions of this Article. Upon the adoption of such a resolution, it shall be certified to the Board of Supervisors of Elections in the county, which Board (pursuant to the election laws of the State) shall submit to the voters of the county at the next ensuing general election the question whether the resolution shall be approved or rejected. If in the referendum a majority of those persons voting on this question vote for the resolution, the resolution is approved, and the county shall become a code county under the provisions of this Article, on the thirtieth day after the election. If in the referendum a majority of those persons voting on this question vote against the resolution, the resolution is rejected, and of no further effect.

Provided that if at the next ensuing general election there shall be submitted to the voters of the county a proposed charter under Article 11A of this Constitution, the proposed charter only shall be submitted to the voters at that next ensuing general election. If the proposed charter is adopted by the voters, this particular resolution to become a code county shall not be submitted to the voters and shall have no further effect. If the proposed charter is rejected by the voters, the code question under this Article shall be submitted to the voters at the general election two years later, and no charter question under Article 11A shall be submitted to the voters at that general election.

SECTION 3. Except as otherwise provided in this Article, a code county may enact, amend, or repeal a public local law of that county, following the procedure in this Article.

SECTION 4. Except as otherwise provided in this Article, the General Assembly shall not enact, amend, or repeal a public local law which is special or local in its terms or effect within a code county. The General Assembly may enact, amend, or repeal public local laws applicable to code counties only by general enactments which in term and effect apply alike to all code counties in one or more of the classes provided for in Section 5 of this Article.

SECTION 5. The General Assembly, by law, shall classify all code counties by grouping them into not more than four classes based either upon population as determined in the most recent Federal or State census or upon such other criteria as determined by the General Assembly to be appropriate. Not more than one such grouping of code counties into four (or fewer) classes may be in effect at any one time, and the enactment of any grouping of code counties into four (or fewer) classes repeals any other such grouping then in effect. Code counties may be classified only as provided in this section.

SECTION 6. A code county may enact, amend, or repeal a public local law of that county by a resolution of the board of county commissioners. The General Assembly may amplify the provisions of this section by general law in any manner not inconsistent with this Article.

SECTION 7. Any action of a code county in the enactment, amendment, or repeal of a public local law is subject to a referendum of the voters in the county, as in this section provided. The enactment, amendment, or repeal shall be effective unless a petition of the registered voters of the county requires that it be submitted to a referendum of the voters in the county. The General Assembly shall amplify the provisions of this section by general law in any manner not inconsistent with this Article, except that in any event the number of signatures required on such a petition shall not be fewer than five percentum (5%) of the voters in a county registered for county and State elections.

SECTION 8. Notwithstanding any other provisions of this Article, the General Assembly has exclusive power to enact, amend, or repeal any local law for a code county which

(1) authorizes or places a maximum limit upon the rate of property taxes which may be imposed by the code county; or

(2) authorizes or regulates the maximum amount of indebtedness which may be incurred by the code county. Public local laws enacted by the General Assembly under this section prevail over any public local laws enacted by the code county under other sections in this Article.

SECTION 9. A code county shall not levy any type of tax, license fee, franchise tax, or fee which was not in effect or authorized in the code county at the time it came under the provisions of this Article, until an express authorization of the General Assembly has been enacted for this purpose by a general law which in its terms and effect applies alike to all code counties in one or more of the classes provided for in Section 5 of this Article.

SECTION 10. All laws enacted by the General Assembly and in effect when this Article was added to the Constitution shall remain in effect until amended or repealed under the Constitution. Every public local law enacted, amended, or repealed by a county under the provisions of this Article prevails over the previous public local law, except to the extent it is subject to an applicable law enacted by the General Assembly.

ARTICLE XI-G: CITY OF BALTIMORE - RESIDENTIAL REHABILITATION AND COMMERCIAL FINANCING LOANS

Section 1. The General Assembly of Maryland, by public local law, may authorize the Mayor and City Council of Baltimore:

(a) To make or contract to make financial loans to any person or other legal entity to be used for or in connection with the rehabilitation, renovation, redevelopment or improvement of buildings or structures located within the boundaries of Baltimore City, which buildings or structures are to be used or occupied for residential purposes.

(b) To guarantee or insure financial loans made by third parties to any person or other legal entity to be used for or in connection with the rehabilitation, renovation, redevelopment or improvement of buildings or structures located within the boundaries of Baltimore City, which buildings or structures are to be used or occupied for residential purposes.

(c) To make or contract to make financial loans to any person or other legal entity to be used for or in connection with the purchase or acquisition of leasehold or fee simple interests in buildings or structures, and for construction, reconstruction, erection, development, rehabilitation, renovation, redevelopment or improvement of buildings or structures, located within the boundaries of Baltimore City, which buildings or structures are to be used or occupied for commercial purposes.

(d) To guarantee or insure financial loans made by third parties to any person or other legal entity to be used for or in connection with the purchase or acquisition of leasehold or fee simple interests in buildings or structures, and for construction, reconstruction, erection, development, rehabilitation, renovation, redevelopment or improvement of buildings or structures, located within the boundaries of Baltimore City, which buildings or structures are to be used or occupied for commercial purposes.

(e) Any and all financial loans made by the Mayor and City Council of Baltimore; any and all guarantees or insurance commitments made by the Mayor and City Council of Baltimore in connection with any of said loans; and any and all money used or expended by the Mayor and City Council of Baltimore in connection with said loans, guarantees, or insurance commitments, pursuant to the power and authority hereinabove vested in the municipality, and any and all acts performed by the Mayor and City Council of Baltimore in connection with any powers which may be granted to the Mayor and City Council of Baltimore pursuant to this Article, are all hereby declared to be needed, contracted for, expended or exercised for a public use.

(f) In the event of any conflict between the provisions of this Article and those of Article XI, Section 7, of the Constitution of Maryland, or any other provisions of said Constitution, then the provisions of this Article shall control.

2. The General Assembly of Maryland may grant to the Mayor and City Council of Baltimore any and all additional power and authority necessary or proper to carry into full force and effect any and all of the specific powers which the General Assembly is authorized to grant to the Mayor and City Council of Baltimore pursuant to this Article, and to fully accomplish any and all of the purposes and objects contemplated by the provisions of this Article, provided such additional power or authority is not inconsistent with the terms and provisions of this Article or with any other provision or provisions of the Constitution of Maryland, except as provided in this Article. The General Assembly may place such other and further restrictions or limitations on the exercise of any of the powers which it may grant to the Mayor and City Council of Baltimore under the provisions of this Article as it may deem proper and expedient.

ARTICLE XI-H: CITY OF BALTIMORE - RESIDENTIAL FINANCING LOANS

Section 1. The General Assembly of Maryland, by public local law, may authorize the Mayor and City Council of Baltimore:

(a) To make or contract to make financial loans to any person or other legal entity to be used for or in connection with the purchase, acquisition, construction, erection or development of buildings or structures, including any land necessary therefor, within the boundaries of Baltimore City, which buildings or structures are to be used or occupied for residential purposes.

(b) To guarantee or insure financial loans made by third parties to any person or other legal entity which are to be used for or in connection with the purchase, acquisition, construction, erection or development of buildings or structures, including any land necessary therefor, within the boundaries of Baltimore City, which buildings or structures are to be used or occupied for residential purposes.

(c) Any and all financial loans made by the Mayor and City Council of Baltimore; any and all guarantees or insurance commitments made by the Mayor and City Council of Baltimore in connection with any of the loans; and any and all money used or expended by the Mayor and City Council of Baltimore in connection with the loans, guarantees, or insurance commitments, pursuant to the power and authority hereinabove vested in the municipality, and any and all acts performed by the Mayor and City Council of Baltimore in connection with any powers which may be granted to the Mayor and City Council of Baltimore pursuant to this Article, are all declared to be needed, contracted for, expended or exercised for a public use.

(d) In the event of any conflict between the provisions of this Article and those of Article XI, Section 7, of the Constitution of Maryland, or any other provisions of the Constitution, then the provisions of this Article shall control.

2. The General Assembly of Maryland may grant to the Mayor and City Council of Baltimore any and all additional power and authority necessary or proper to carry into full force and effect any and all of the specific powers which the General Assembly of Maryland is authorized to grant to the Mayor and City Council of Baltimore pursuant to this Article, and to fully accomplish any and all of the purposes and objects contemplated by the provisions of this Article, provided such additional power or authority is not inconsistent with the terms and provisions of this Article or with any other provision or provisions of the Constitution of Maryland, except as provided in this Article. The General Assembly may place such other and further restrictions or limitations on the exercise of any of the powers which it may grant to the Mayor and City Council of Baltimore under the provisions of this Article as it may deem proper and expedient.

ARTICLE XI-I: CITY OF BALTIMORE - INDUSTRIAL FINANCING LOANS

Section 1. The General Assembly of Maryland, by public local law, may authorize the Mayor and City Council of Baltimore:

(a) To make or contract to make financial loans to any person or other legal entity to be used for or in connection with the purchase, acquisition, construction, reconstruction, erection, development, redevelopment, rehabilitation, renovation, modernization or improvement of buildings or structures, including any land necessary therefor, within the boundaries of Baltimore City, which buildings or structures are to be used or occupied for industrial purposes.

(b) To guarantee or insure financial loans made by third parties to any person or other legal entity which are to be used for or in connection with the purchase, acquisition, construction, reconstruction, erection, development, redevelopment, rehabilitation, renovation, modernization, or improvement of buildings or structures, including any land necessary therefor, within the boundaries of Baltimore City, which buildings or structures are to be used or occupied for industrial purposes.

(c) Any and all financial loans made by the Mayor and City Council of Baltimore; any and all guarantees or insurance commitments made by the Mayor and City Council of Baltimore in connection with any of the loans; and any and all money used or expended by the Mayor and City Council of Baltimore in connection with the loans, guarantees, or insurance commitments, pursuant to the power and

authority hereinabove vested in the municipality, and any and all acts performed by the Mayor and City Council of Baltimore in connection with any powers which may be granted to the Mayor and City Council of Baltimore pursuant to this Article, are all declared to be needed, contracted for, expended or exercised for a public use.
(d) In the event of any conflict between the provisions of this Article and those of Article XI, Section 7, of the Constitution of Maryland, or any other provisions of the Constitution, then the provisions of this Article shall control.

2. The General Assembly of Maryland may grant to the Mayor and City Council of Baltimore any and all additional power and authority necessary or proper to carry into full force and effect any and all of the specific powers which the General Assembly of Maryland is authorized to grant to the Mayor and City Council of Baltimore pursuant to this Article, and to fully accomplish any and all of the purposes and objects contemplated by the provisions of this Article, provided such additional power or authority is not inconsistent with the terms and provisions of this Article or with any other provision or provisions of the Constitution of Maryland, except as provided in this Article. The General Assembly may place such other and further restrictions or limitations on the exercise of any of the powers which it may grant to the Mayor and City Council of Baltimore under the provisions of this Article as it may deem proper and expedient.

ARTICLE XII: PUBLIC WORKS

SECTION 1. The Governor, the Comptroller of the Treasury and the Treasurer, shall constitute the Board of Public Works in this State. They shall keep a journal of their proceedings, and shall hold regular sessions in the City of Annapolis, on the first Wednesday in January, April, July and October, in each year, and oftener, if necessary; at which sessions they shall hear and determine such matters as affect the Public Works of the State, and as the General Assembly may confer upon them the power to decide.

SECTION 2. They shall exercise a diligent and faithful supervision of all Public Works in which the State may be interested as Stockholder or Creditor, and shall appoint the Directors in every Railroad and Canal Company, in which the State has the legal power to appoint Directors, which said Directors shall represent the State in all meetings of the Stockholders of the respective Companies for which they are appointed or elected. They shall require the Directors of all said Public Works to guard the public interest, and prevent the establishment of tolls which shall discriminate against the interest of the citizens or products of this State, and from time to time, and as often as there shall be any change in the rates of toll on any of the said Works, to furnish the said Board of Public Works a schedule of such modified rates of toll, and so adjust them as to promote the agricultural interests of the State; they shall report to the General Assembly at each regular session, and recommend such legislation as they may deem necessary and requisite to promote or protect the interests of the State in the said Public Works; they shall perform such other duties as may be hereafter prescribed by Law, and a majority of them shall be competent to act. The Governor,

Comptroller and Treasurer shall receive no additional salary for services rendered by them as members of the Board of Public Works.

SECTION 3.

(a) The Board of Public Works is hereby authorized, subject to such regulations and conditions as the General Assembly may from time to time prescribe, to sell the State's interest in all works of Internal Improvement, whether as a stockholder or a creditor, and also the State's interest in any banking corporation, receiving in payment the bonds and registered debt now owing by the State, equal in amount to the price obtained for the State's said interest.

(b) The Board of Public Works may not approve the sale, transfer, exchange, grant, or other permanent disposition of any State-owned outdoor recreation, open space, conservation, preservation, forest, or park land without the express approval of the General Assembly or of a committee that the General Assembly designates by statute, resolution, or rule.

ARTICLE XIII: NEW COUNTIES

SECTION 1. The General Assembly may provide, by Law, for organizing new Counties, locating and removing county seats, and changing county lines; but no new county shall be organized without the consent of the majority of the legal voters residing within the limits proposed to be formed into said new county; and whenever a new county shall be proposed to be formed out of portions of two or more counties, the consent of a majority of the legal voters of such part of each of said counties, respectively, shall be required; nor shall the lines of any county nor of Baltimore City be changed without the consent of a majority of the legal voters residing within the district, which under said proposed change, would form a part of a county or of Baltimore City different from that to which it belonged prior to said change; and no new county shall contain less than four hundred square miles, nor less than ten thousand inhabitants; nor shall any change be made in the limits of any county, whereby the population of said county would be reduced to less than ten thousand inhabitants, or its territory reduced to less than four hundred square miles. No county lines heretofore validly established shall be changed except in accordance with this section.

SECTION 2. The General Assembly shall pass all such Laws as may be necessary more fully to carry into effect the provisions of this Article.

ARTICLE XIV: AMENDMENTS TO THE CONSTITUTION

SECTION 1. The General Assembly may propose Amendments to this Constitution; provided that each Amendment shall be embraced in a separate bill, embodying the Article or Section, as the same will stand when amended and passed by three-fifths of all the members elected to each of the two Houses, by yeas and nays, to be entered on the Journals with the proposed Amendment. The requirement in this section that an amendment proposed by the General Assembly shall be embraced in a separate bill shall not be construed or applied to prevent the General Assembly from (1) proposing in one bill a series of amendments to the Constitution of Maryland for the general purpose of removing or correcting constitutional provisions which are obsolete, inaccurate, invalid, unconstitutional, or duplicative; or (2) embodying in a single Constitutional amendment one or more Articles of the Constitution so long as that Constitutional amendment embraces only a single subject. The bill or bills proposing amendment or amendments shall be publicized, either by publishing, by order of the Governor, in at least two newspapers, in each County, where so many may be published, and where not more than one may be published, then in that newspaper, and in three newspapers published in the City of Baltimore, once a week for four weeks, or as otherwise ordered by the Governor in a manner provided by law, immediately preceding the next ensuing general election, at which the proposed amendment or amendments shall be submitted, in a form to be prescribed by the General Assembly, to the qualified voters of the State for adoption or rejection. The votes cast for and against said proposed amendment or amendments, severally, shall be returned to the Governor, in the manner prescribed in other cases, and if it shall appear to the Governor that a majority of the votes cast at said election on said amendment or amendments, severally, were cast in favor thereof, the Governor shall, by his proclamation, declare the said amendment or amendments having received said majority of votes, to have been adopted by the people of Maryland as part of the Constitution thereof, and thenceforth said amendment or amendments shall be part of the said Constitution. If the General Assembly determines that a proposed Constitutional amendment affects only one county or the City of Baltimore, the proposed amendment shall be part of the Constitution if it receives a majority of the votes cast in the State and in the affected county or City of Baltimore, as the case may be. When two or more amendments shall be submitted to the voters of this State at the same election, they shall be so submitted as that each amendment shall be voted on separately.

SECTION 1A A proposed Constitutional amendment which, by provisions that are of limited duration, provides for a period of transition, or a unique schedule under which the terms of the amendment are to become effective, shall set forth those provisions in the amendment as a section or sections of a separate article, to be known as "provisions of limited duration", and state the date upon which or the circumstances under which those provisions shall expire. If the Constitutional amendment is adopted, those provisions of limited duration shall have the same force and effect as any other part of the Constitution, except that they shall remain a part of the Constitution only so long as their terms require. Each new section of the article known as "provisions of limited duration" shall refer to the title and section of the other article of the Constitution of which it, temporarily, is a part.

SECTION 2. It shall be the duty of the General Assembly to provide by Law for taking, at the general election to be held in the year nineteen hundred and seventy, and every twenty years thereafter, the sense of the People in regard to calling a Convention for altering this Constitution; and if a majority of voters at such election or elections shall vote for a Convention, the General Assembly, at its next session, shall provide by Law for the assembling of such convention, and for the election of Delegates thereto. Each County, and Legislative District of the City of Baltimore, shall have in such Convention a number of Delegates equal to its representation in both Houses at the time at which the Convention is called. But any Constitution, or change, or amendment of the existing Constitution, which may be adopted by such Convention, shall be submitted to the voters of this State, and shall have no effect unless the same shall have been adopted by a majority of the voters voting thereon.

ARTICLE XV: MISCELLANEOUS

SECTION 1. Every person holding any office created by, or existing under the Constitution, or Laws of the State, or holding any appointment under any Court of this State, whose pay, or compensation is derived from fees, or moneys coming into his hands for the discharge of his official duties, or, in any way, growing out of, or connected with his office, shall keep a book in which shall be entered every sum, or sums of money, received by him, or on his account, as a payment or compensation for his performance of official duties, a copy of which entries in said book, verified by the oath of the officer, by whom it is directed to be kept, shall be returned yearly to the Comptroller of the State for his inspection, and that of the General Assembly of the State, to which the Comptroller shall, at each regular session thereof, make a report showing what officers have complied with this Section; and each of the said officers, when the amount received by him for the year shall exceed the sum which he is by Law entitled to retain, as his salary or compensation for the discharge of his duties, and for the expenses of his office, shall yearly pay over to the Treasurer of the State the amount of such excess, subject to such disposition thereof as the General Assembly may direct; if any of such officers shall fail to comply with the requisitions of this section for the period of thirty days after the expiration of each and every year of his office, such officer shall be deemed to have vacated his office, and the Governor shall declare the same vacant, and the vacancy therein shall be filled as in the case of vacancy for any other cause, and such officer shall be subject to suit by the State for the amount that ought to be paid into the Treasury.

SECTION 2. Any elected official of the State, or of a county or of a municipal corporation who during the elected official's term of office is found guilty of any crime which is a felony, or which is a misdemeanor related to the elected official's public duties and responsibilities and involves moral turpitude for which the penalty may be incarceration in any penal institution, shall be suspended by operation of law without pay or benefits from the elective office. During and for the period of suspension of the elected official, the appropriate governing body and/ or official authorized by law to fill any vacancy in the elective office shall appoint a person to temporarily fill the elective office, provided that if the elective office is one for which automatic succession is provided by law, then in such event the person entitled to succeed to the office shall temporarily fill the elective office. If the finding of guilt becomes a final conviction, after judicial review or otherwise, such elected official shall be removed from the elective office by operation of Law and the office shall be deemed vacant. If the finding of guilt of the elected official is reversed or overturned, the elected official shall be reinstated by operation of Law to the elective office for the remainder, if any, of the elective term of office during which the elected official was removed, and all pay and benefits shall be restored. Any elected official of the State, or of a county or of a municipal corporation who during the elected official's term of office enters a guilty plea or a plea of nolo contendere to any crime which is a felony, or which is misdemeanor related to the elected official's public duties and responsibilities and involves moral turpitude for which the penalty may be incarceration in any penal institution, shall be removed from the elective office by operation of law and the office shall be deemed vacant.

SECTION 3. No person who is a member of an organization that advocates the overthrow of the Government of the United States or of the State of Maryland through force or violence shall be eligible to hold any office, be it elective or appointive, or any other position of profit or trust in the Government of or in the administration of the business of this State or of any county, municipality or other political subdivision of this State.

SECTION 4. Vacant.

SECTION 5. Except as the Constitution provides otherwise for any office, the General Assembly may provide by law for a person to act in place of any elected or appointed officer of the State who is unavailable to perform the duties of his office because he has become unable or is or will be absent.

SECTION 6. Vacant.

SECTION 7. All general elections in this State shall be held on the Tuesday next after the first Monday in the month of November, in the year in which they shall occur.

SECTION 8. Vacant.

SECTION 9. Vacant.

SECTION 10. Vacant.

SECTION 11. Vacant.

ARTICLE XVI: THE REFERENDUM

SECTION 1.

(a) The people reserve to themselves power known as The Referendum, by petition to have submitted to the registered voters of the State, to approve or reject at the polls, any Act, or part of any Act of the General Assembly, if approved by the Governor, or, if passed by the General Assembly over the veto of the Governor;

(b) The provisions of this Article shall be self-executing; provided that additional legislation in furtherance thereof and not in conflict therewith may be enacted.

SECTION 2. No law enacted by the General Assembly shall take effect until the first day of June next after the session at which it may be passed, unless it contains a Section declaring such law an emergency law and necessary for the immediate preservation of the public health or safety and is passed upon a yea and nay vote supported by three-fifths of all the members elected to each of the two Houses of the General Assembly. The effective date of a law other than an emergency law may be extended as provided in Section 3 (b) hereof. If before said first day of June there shall have been filed with the Secretary of the State a petition to refer to a vote of the people any law or part of a law capable of referendum, as in this Article provided, the same shall be referred by the Secretary of State to such vote, and shall not become a law or take effect until thirty days after its approval by a majority of the electors voting thereon at the next ensuing election held throughout the State for Members of the House of Representatives of the United States. An emergency law shall remain in force notwithstanding such petition, but shall stand repealed thirty days after having been rejected by a majority of the qualified electors voting thereon. No measure changing the salary of any officer, or granting any franchise or special privilege, or creating any vested right or interest, shall be enacted as an emergency law. No law making any appropriation for maintaining the State Government, or for maintaining or aiding any public institution, not exceeding the next previous appropriation for the same purpose, shall be subject to rejection or repeal under this Section. The increase in any such appropriation for maintaining or aiding any public institution shall only take effect as in the case of other laws, and such increase or any part thereof specified in the petition, may be referred to a vote of the people upon petition.

SECTION 3.

(a) The referendum petition against an Act or part of an Act passed by the General Assembly, shall be sufficient if signed by three percent of the qualified voters of the State of Maryland, calculated upon the whole number of votes cast for Governor at the last preceding Gubernatorial election, of whom not more than half are residents of Baltimore City, or of any one County. However, any Public Local Law for any one County or the City of Baltimore, shall be referred by the Secretary of State only to the people of the County or City of Baltimore, upon a referendum petition of ten percent of the qualified voters of the County or City of Baltimore, as the case may be, calculated upon the whole number of votes cast respectively for Governor at the last preceding Gubernatorial election.

(b) If more than one-third, but less than the full number of signatures required to complete any referendum petition against any law passed by the General Assembly, be filed with the Secretary of State before the first day of June, the time for the law to take effect and for filing the remainder of signatures to complete the petition shall be extended to the thirtieth day of the same month, with like effect.
If an Act is passed less than 45 days prior to June 1, it may not become effective sooner than 31 days after its passage. To bring this Act to referendum, the first one-third of the required number of signatures to a petition shall be submitted within 30 days after its passage. If the first one-third of the required number of signatures is submitted to the Secretary of State within 30 days after its passage, the time for the Act to take effect and for filing the remainder of the signatures to complete the petition shall be extended for an additional 30 days.

(c) In this Article, "pass" or "passed" means any final action upon any Act or part of an Act by both Houses of the General Assembly; and "enact" or "enacted" means approval of an Act or part of an Act by the Governor.

(d) Signatures on a petition for referendum on an Act or part of an Act may be signed at any time after the Act or part of an Act is passed.

SECTION 4. A petition may consist of several papers, but each paper shall contain the full text, or an accurate summary approved by the Attorney General, of the Act or part of Act petitioned. There shall be attached to each paper of signatures filed with a petition an affidavit of the person procuring those signatures that the signatures were affixed in his presence and that, based upon the person's best knowledge and belief, every signature on the paper is genuine and bona fide and that the signers are registered voters at the address set opposite or below their names. The General Assembly shall prescribe by law the form of the petition, the manner for verifying its authenticity, and other administrative procedures which facilitate the petition process and which are not in conflict with this Article.

SECTION 5.

(a) The General Assembly shall provide for furnishing the voters of the State the text of all measures to be voted upon by the people; provided, that until otherwise provided by law the same shall be published in the manner prescribed by Article XIV of the Constitution for the publication of proposed Constitutional Amendments.

(b) All laws referred under the provisions of this Article shall be submitted separately on the ballots to the voters of the people, but if containing more than two hundred words, the full text shall not be printed on the official ballots, but the Secretary of State shall prepare and submit a ballot title of each such measure in such form as to present the purpose of said measure concisely and intelligently. The ballot title may be distinct from the legislative title, but in any case the legislative title shall be sufficient. Upon each of the ballots, following the ballot title or text, as the case may be, of each such measure, there shall be printed the words "For the referred law" and "Against the referred law," as the case may be. The votes cast for and against any such referred law shall be returned to the Governor in the manner prescribed with respect to proposed amendments to the Constitution under Article XIV of this Constitution, and the Governor shall proclaim the result of the election, and, if it shall appear that the majority of the votes cast on any such measure were cast in favor thereof, the Governor shall by his proclamation declare the same having received a majority of the votes to have been adopted by the people of Maryland as a part of the laws of the State, to take effect thirty days after such election, and in like manner and with like effect the Governor shall proclaim the result of the local election as to any Public Local Law which shall have been submitted to the voters of any County or of the City of Baltimore.

SECTION 6. No law, licensing, regulating, prohibiting, or submitting to local option, the manufacture or sale of malt or spirituous liquors, shall be referred or repealed under the provisions of this Article.

ARTICLE XVII: QUADRENNIAL ELECTIONS

SECTION 1. The purpose of this Article is to reduce the number of elections by providing that all State and county elections shall be held only in every fourth year, and at the time provided by law for holding congressional elections, and to bring the terms of appointive officers into harmony with the changes effected in the time of the beginning of the terms of elective officers. The administrative and judicial officers of the State shall construe the provisions of this Article so as to effectuate that purpose. For the purpose of this Article only the word "officers" shall be construed to include those holding positions and other places of employment in the State and county governments whose terms are fixed by law, but it shall not include any appointments made by the Board of Public Works, nor appointments by the Governor for terms of three years.

SECTION 2. Except for a special election that may be authorized to fill a vacancy in a County Council or a vacancy in the office of chief executive officer or County Executive, under Article XI-A, Section 3 of the Constitution, elections by qualified voters for State and county officers shall be held on the Tuesday next after the first Monday of November, in the year nineteen hundred and twenty-six, and on the same day in every fourth year thereafter.

SECTION 3. All State and county officers elected by qualified voters (except judges of the Circuit Courts, judges of the Supreme Bench of Baltimore City, judges of the Court of Appeals and judges of any intermediate courts of appeal) shall hold office for terms of four years, and until their successors shall qualify.

SECTION 4. The term of office of all Judges and other officers, for whose election provision is made by this Constitution, shall, except in cases otherwise expressly provided herein, commence from the time of their Election. All such officers shall qualify as soon after their election as practicable, and shall enter upon the duties of their respective offices immediately upon their qualification.

SECTION 5. All officers to be appointed by the Governor shall hold office for the terms fixed by law. All officers appointed by County Commissioners shall hold office for terms of four years, unless otherwise duly changed by law.

SECTION 6. The terms of the Members of the Board of Supervisors of Elections of Baltimore City and of the several counties shall commence on the first Monday of June next ensuing their appointment.

SECTION 7. Sections 1, 2, 3, and 5 of this Article do not apply or refer to: (1) members of any elective local board of education; or (2) the Board of County Commissioners for Cecil County.

SECTION 8. If at any election directed by this Constitution, any two or more candidates shall have the highest and an equal number of votes, a new election shall be ordered by the Governor, except in cases specially provided for by this Constitution.

SECTION 9. In the event of any inconsistency between the provisions of this Article and any of the other provisions of the Constitution, the provisions of this Article shall prevail, and all other provisions shall be repealed or abrogated to the extent of such inconsistency.

SECTION 10. Vacant.

SECTION 11. Vacant.

SECTION 12. Vacant.

SECTION 13. Vacant.

ARTICLE XVIII: PROVISIONS OF LIMITED DURATION

SECTION 1. Any provision of limited duration adopted pursuant to Article XIV is set forth below. As each expires, it shall stand repealed, and no further action shall be required to remove it from the Constitution.

SECTION 2. Vacant.

SECTION 3. Of the methods of election of county commissioners authorized by Section 1 of Article VII, and of members of county councils authorized by Section 3A(a) of Article XI-A, of this Act, that method in effect in each county immediately preceding the effective date of this Act shall remain in effect unless changed on or after that date pursuant to this Constitution.

SECTION 4.

(a) For the purpose of implementing the amendment proposed by House Bill 635 of 1994 concerning the boundaries of the appellate judicial circuits from which members of the Court of Appeals are appointed, this section temporarily is part of Article IV - Judiciary Department, Section 14 of the Constitution. This section shall expire, in accordance with Article XIV, Section 1A of the Constitution, when under the provisions of subsections (b), (c), (d), and (e) of this section, all of the judges of the Court of Appeals on January 12, 1994, or their successors appointed before the effective date of House Bill 635 of 1994 have vacated their offices.

(b) Except as provided in subsection (d) of this section, the provisions of House Bill 635 of 1994 may not be construed to limit or otherwise affect the terms or appointments of the judges of the Court of Appeals who are in office on the effective date of House Bill 635 of 1994.

(c) The judges of the Court of Appeals in office on January 12, 1994, or their successors, shall be deemed to be serving appointments as follows:

(1) Judge Robert L. Karwacki of Queen Anne's County and currently representing the First Appellate Judicial Circuit, shall continue on the Court as an appointee from the new First Appellate Judicial Circuit;

(2) Judge Robert C. Murphy of Baltimore County and currently representing the Second Appellate Judicial Circuit, shall continue on the Court as an appointee from the Second Appellate Judicial Circuit;

(3) Judge John C. Eldridge of Anne Arundel County and currently representing the Fifth Appellate Judicial Circuit, shall continue on the Court as an appointee from the new Fifth Appellate Judicial Circuit;

(4) Judge Howard S. Chasanow of Prince George's County and currently representing the Fourth Appellate Judicial Circuit, shall continue on the Court as an appointee from the new Fourth Appellate Judicial Circuit;

(5) Judge Irma S. Raker of Montgomery County and currently representing the Third Appellate Judicial Circuit, shall continue on the Court as an appointee from the new Seventh Appellate Judicial Circuit;

(6) Judge Robert M. Bell of Baltimore City and currently representing the Sixth Appellate Judicial Circuit, shall continue on the Court as an appointee from the Sixth Appellate Judicial Circuit; and

(7) Judge Lawrence F. Rodowsky of Baltimore City and currently representing the Sixth Judicial Circuit, shall continue on the Court as an appointee from the new Third Appellate Judicial Circuit.

(d) An appointment to fill a vacancy on the Court of Appeals, following the adoption of the amendment proposed by House Bill 635 of 1994 by the voters of this State in accordance with the provisions of Article XIV of the Constitution of the State, shall be made in accordance with the provisions of Article IV, Section 14 of the Constitution of the State.

(e) Each judge of the Court of Appeals in office on January 12, 1994, or the judge's successor, shall be eligible to continue to serve on the Court:

(1) In accordance with the provisions of subsection (c) of this Section; and

(2) Upon election from the new circuits established under Article IV, Section 14 of the Constitution of the State following the adoption of the amendment proposed by House Bill 635 of 1994 by the voters of this State in accordance with the provisions of Article XIV of the Constitution of the State, except that Judge Lawrence F. Rodowsky of Baltimore City, if otherwise eligible to continue to serve on the Court but for his lack of residence in the new Third Appellate Judicial Circuit, shall be eligible to continue to serve on the Court upon election statewide.

SECTION 5.

(a) For the purpose of implementing the amendments proposed by House Bill 916 of 1995 concerning the membership of the Commission on Judicial Disabilities, this section temporarily is part of Article IV - Judiciary Department, Section 4A of the Constitution. This section shall expire, in accordance with Article XIV, Section 1A of the Constitution, when the terms of the members initially appointed to fill the five new memberships added to the Commission under House Bill 916 of 1995 have expired in accordance with subsection (b) of this section.

(b) (1) The initial terms of the four members of the public added to the Commission under House Bill 916 of 1995 shall expire as follows:

(i) Two members in 1999, and each of those members may be appointed to two full terms; and

(ii) Two members in 2000, and each of those members may be appointed to one full term.

(2) The initial term of the member of the Bar added to the Commission under House Bill 916 of 1995 shall expire in 1998.

(c) For the purpose of implementing the elimination of one of the four judicial memberships, the following provisions apply:

(1) If a vacancy exists in a judicial membership at the time the Governor issues the proclamation under Article XIV, Section 1 of the Constitution, declaring the amendments proposed by House Bill 916 of 1995 to have been adopted, a successor may not be appointed and that membership shall be terminated.

(2) If no vacancy exists in a judicial membership at the time the Governor issues the proclamation under Article XIV, Section 1 of the Constitution, declaring the amendments proposed by House Bil 916 of 1995 to have been adopted, the four judges serving on the Commission may continue to serve. When the first vacancy in a judicial membership occurs, a successor may not be appointed and that membership shall be terminated.

(3) If no vacancy in a judicial membership occurs before January 1, 1999, one of the two judges whose terms expire on January 1, 1999 may not be reappointed and the membership held by that judge shall be terminated.

ARTICLE XIX: VIDEO LOTTERY TERMINALS

SECTION 1.

(a) This article does not apply to:

(1) Lotteries conducted under Title 9, Subtitle 1 of the State Government Article of the Annotated Code of Maryland;

(2) Wagering on horse racing conducted under Title 11 of the Business Regulation Article of the Annotated Code of Maryland; or

(3) Gaming conducted under Title 12 or Title 13 of the Criminal Law Article of the Annotated Code of Maryland.

(b) In this article, "video lottery operation license" means a license issued to a person that allows players to operate video lottery terminals.

(c) (1) Except as provided in subsection (e) of this section, the State may issue up to five video lottery operation licenses throughout the State for the primary purpose of raising revenue for:

(i) Education for the children of the State in public schools, prekindergarten through grade 12;

(ii) Public school construction and public school capital improvements; and

(iii) Construction of capital projects at community colleges and public senior higher education institutions.

(2) Except as provided in subsection (e) of this section, the State may not authorize the operation of more than 15,000 video lottery terminals in the State.

(3) Except as provided in subsection (e) of this section, a video lottery operation license only may be awarded for a video lottery facility in the following locations:

(i) Anne Arundel County, within 2 miles of MD Route 295;

(ii) Cecil County, within 2 miles of Interstate 95;

(iii) Worcester County, within 1 mile of the intersection of Route 50 and Route 589;

(iv) On State property located within Rocky Gap State Park in Allegany County; or

(v) Baltimore City, if the video lottery facility is:

1. Located:

A. In a nonresidential area;

B. Within one-half mile of Interstate 95;

C. Within one-half mile of MD Route 295; and

D. On property that is owned by Baltimore City on the date on which the application for a video lottery operation license is submitted; and

2. Not adjacent to or within one-quarter mile of property that is:

A. Zoned for residential use; and

B. Used for a residential dwelling on the date the application for a video lottery operation license is submitted.

(4) Except as provided in subsection (e) of this section, the State may not award more than one video lottery operation license in a single county or Baltimore City.

(5) A video lottery facility shall comply with all applicable planning and zoning laws of the local jurisdiction.

(d) Except as provided in subsection (e) of this section, on or after November 15, 2008, the General Assembly may not authorize any additional forms or expansion of commercial gaming.

(e) The General Assembly may only authorize additional forms or expansion of commercial gaming if approval is granted through a referendum, authorized by an act of the General Assembly, in a general election by a majority of the qualified voters in the State.

(f) The General Assembly may, from time to time, enact such laws not inconsistent with this section, as may be necessary and proper to carry out its provisions.